# Table of Contents

# Chapter 1
# Avian Adventures

☐ **1.** The Superb Lyrebird, native to Australia, has the most complex syrinx (vocal organ) of any songbird, enabling it to mimic a wide array of sounds, including chainsaws and camera shutters.

☐ **2.** Peregrine Falcons, known for their incredible speed, can dive at speeds exceeding 240 miles per hour.

☐ **3.** The Houtzin, found in the Amazon rainforest, is nicknamed the "stinkbird" due to its foul odor, reminiscent of fermenting fruit, emanating from its digestive system. Young Houtzins are known for having claws on their wings, which help them climb tree branches.

☐ **4.** Kakapos, flightless parrots from New Zealand, are the heaviest parrot species globally and can weigh up to 9 pounds. They are nocturnal, which means they are primarily active during the night.

☐ **5.** The Flamingo's pink hue comes from its diet rich in carotenoids found in algae and crustaceans. Its long, spindly legs allow it to effortlessly wade through shallow waters.

☐ **6.** The Eurasian Roller performs stunning aerial acrobatics during courtship displays, soaring high into the sky before plummeting toward the ground in a series of twists and turns.

☐ **7.** Toucans have vibrant, oversized bills that, despite their appearance, are surprisingly lightweight due to a network of air pockets within them.

☐ **8.** Native to New Zealand, the Kiwi is a flightless bird that lays one of the largest eggs. The eggs can weigh more than a pound, and the shells are teal, emerald, or dark green.

☐ **9.** The Potoo, with its wide eyes and cryptic plumage, resembles a tree stump during the day, blending seamlessly into its surroundings to avoid predators.

☐ **10.** Ostriches are the largest living birds. They have eyes bigger than their brains and can run at speeds of more than 40 miles per hour, making them one of the fastest runners in the animal kingdom.

☐ **11.** The Bee Hummingbird, found in Cuba, is the smallest bird in the world. Weighing less than a penny, its wings flap at an astonishing rate of up to 80 times per second.

☐ **12.** Shoebill storks, with their prehistoric appearance and massive, shoe-shaped bills, are known for their silent hunting technique. They strike with lightning speed to catch prey.

☐ **13.** The Satin Bowerbird, native to Australia, constructs elaborate bowers adorned with blue objects to attract mates, demonstrating remarkable architectural and artistic skills.

☐ **14.** The Kea, a New Zealand parrot, is notorious for its mischievous behavior, often stealing shiny objects from campsites and even vandalizing cars.

☐ **15.** Snowy Owls, native to the Arctic tundra, have densely feathered feet that act as natural snowshoes, enabling them to hunt effectively in snowy conditions.

☐ **16.** The Malleefowl, native to Australia, builds massive mounds of decaying vegetation to incubate its eggs, using the heat generated by the composting material to regulate the temperature of the eggs.

☐ **17.** The African Grey Parrot possesses exceptional cognitive abilities, with some individuals demonstrating vocabulary and problem-solving skills comparable to a young child.

☐ **18.** Hummingbirds are the only birds able to hover and fly backward, which is due to their rapid wing beats of more than 50 times per second and their unique shoulder joints.

☐ **19.** The Black Skimmer, with its unique uneven bill, in which the lower bill is longer than its upper bill, flies low over the water, dipping its lower mandible in the water to catch fish.

☐ **20.** Emus, native to Australia, are excellent swimmers and one of the fastest birds, running at speeds reaching 30 miles per hour.

☐ **21.** The Maleo, found in Indonesia, lays its eggs in volcanic sand and relies on the heat from geothermal sources to incubate them, demonstrating an extraordinary adaptation to its environment.

☐ **22.** The Galápagos Albatross performs elaborate courtship dances with its mate, consisting of synchronized head movements and bill clacking, strengthening their pair bond.

☐ **23.** The Hoopoe, known for its distinctive crown of feathers, has a unique feeding behavior of probing its long, slender bill into the ground to extract insects and larvae.

☐ **24.** The Northern Gannet, renowned for its spectacular diving abilities, plunges to depths of more than 70 feet in search of fish.

☐ **25.** The Inca Tern, with its striking mustache-like white feathers, performs intricate aerial displays during courtship, showcasing its agility and grace in flight.

# **Bonus**Facts

Owls have specialized feathers and wing structures that enable them to fly silently. This stealthy flight allows them to sneak up on prey without being heard, giving them a hunting advantage in the darkness of night.

Albatrosses are master long-distance flyers, capable of traveling thousands of miles without rest. Some species have been known to circumnavigate the globe in just a few months, using ocean winds to glide effortlessly for hours on end.

Crows are highly intelligent birds known for their problem-solving abilities. They can use tools to obtain food, recognize human faces, and even engage in playful behavior like sliding down snowy slopes for fun.

 **Check the box next to the facts that are your favorites or that you would like to learn more about.**

# Chapter 2
# Magnificent Mammals

☐ **1.** A Narwhal's long tusk, resembling a unicorn horn, is actually an elongated tooth. Scientists still debate their purpose, but they may be used for communication or breaking through icy waters.

☐ **2.** Otters are skilled tool users. They use rocks to crack open shellfish, and sometimes even keep a favorite rock in a pouch of skin under their arm for safekeeping.

☐ **3.** Sloths are the ultimate chill mammals. They move so slowly that their fur gets covered in algae, providing camouflage. They spend up to 20 hours a day sleeping and move at a leisurely pace of around 0.15 miles per hour.

☐ **4.** Seal whiskers are incredibly sensitive, helping them detect vibrations and movements in the water. They can even sense the ripples created by a fish swimming up to 150 feet away.

☐ **5.** An elephant's trunk has remarkable dexterity. It can pick up tiny objects, suck up water for drinking or spraying, and even trumpet loudly to communicate.

☐ **6.** Male humpback whales sing complex songs lasting up to 20 minutes and travel thousands of miles underwater. These songs may be used for communication, attracting mates, or establishing territory.

☐ **7.** Dolphins are incredibly fast swimmers, reaching speeds of nearly 40 miles per hour. They use their streamlined bodies and powerful tails to propel themselves through the water with ease.

☐ **8.** Despite appearing white, a polar bear's fur is actually transparent. Each hair is hollow and reflects light, helping the bear blend into its icy surroundings while trapping heat to keep it warm.

☐ **9.** A giraffe's tongue can stretch up to 20 inches long. This helps them reach leaves high up in trees that other animals can't access.

☐ **10.** The whale shark is the largest fish in the world, reaching lengths of up to 60 feet. Despite their massive size, they primarily feed on tiny plankton, filtering them from the water with their wide mouths.

☐ **11.** Kangaroos are exceptional jumpers, capable of hopping up to 30 feet in a single bound and reaching heights of 10 feet. Their hind legs are large and powerful and are used to propel them forward.

☐ **12.** Despite being large mammals, manatees are surprisingly slow swimmers, typically moving at speeds of around 5 miles per hour. Their slow pace is due to their large, bulky bodies and gentle nature.

☐ **13.** Giant pandas spend up to 12 hours a day eating bamboo. Despite being classified as carnivores, their diet consists almost entirely of bamboo, which they have a unique digestive system to break down.

☐ **14.** The blue whale is the largest mammal in the world. It has the largest heart of any animal, weighing approximately 400 pounds. This massive heart pumps blood throughout its enormous body, which can be up to 100 feet long and weigh nearly 200 tons.

☐ **15.** Cheetahs are the fastest land animals. It can go from a standstill to 60 miles per hour in a few seconds. Their incredible speed helps them chase down prey on the African savannah.

☐ **16.** Orangutans are highly intelligent primates, capable of using tools and solving complex problems. They have been seen using sticks to extract insects from trees and constructing makeshift umbrellas from leaves.

☐ **17.** Octopuses are masters of disguise, able to change both their color and texture to blend in with their surroundings. They use specialized cells called chromatophores to achieve this remarkable camouflage.

☐ **18.** Anteaters' tongues can extend up to two feet long. This specialized tongue helps them reach deep into anthills and termite mounds to easily eat insects.

☐ **19.** Beluga whales are sometimes called "canaries of the sea" due to their diverse vocalizations. They can produce a wide diversity of sounds, including whistles, chirps, and clicks, which they use for communication and echolocation.

☐ **20.** The platypus is one of the only mammals that lays eggs. It also has a duck-like bill, webbed feet for swimming, and venomous spurs on its hind legs, making it one of the most unusual animals in the world.

☐ **21.** Wolves are incredibly social animals. They live and hunt in packs and are led by an alpha pair. Each pack has a complex hierarchy, with individuals cooperating to hunt, raise young, and defend territory.

☐ **22.** When threatened, a hedgehog will curl into a small ball, with its spines pointing outward for protection. This defensive posture helps deter predators and keeps the hedgehog safe from harm.

☐ **23.** Moose have the largest antlers of any living deer species, spanning up to six feet wide. These impressive antlers are shed and regrown annually, with larger antlers indicating a healthier and more dominant male.

☐ **24.** Pangolins are covered in tough, overlapping scales made of keratin, the same material found in human hair and nails. When threatened, they curl into a ball, using their tough scales as armor against predators.

☐ **25.** Gorillas are incredibly strong, with adult males capable of lifting up to 4,000 pounds. Despite their immense power, they are generally gentle and peaceful animals, preferring to avoid conflict.

# **Bonus**Facts

Arctic foxes have thick fur coats and small ears to help them survive in cold climates. They also have keen hunting instincts, can locate prey beneath the snow, and can withstand temperatures as low as -58°F.

Koalas primarily feed on eucalyptus leaves, which are toxic to most animals due to their high levels of toxins and low nutritional value. Their specialized digestive systems break down these leaves, allowing them to extract nutrients and survive on this diet.

# Chapter 3
# Rebellious Reptiles

☐ **1.** The basilisk lizard can run on water. With its webbed feet and incredible speed, it can sprint across the surface of ponds and streams, earning it the nickname "Jesus Christ lizard."

☐ **2.** Did you know that some snakes can fly? Well, sort of. The paradise tree snake can flatten its body and glide through the air from tree to tree, making it one of the few "flying" snakes worldwide.

☐ **3.** Unlike humans, who shed skin cells constantly, snakes shed their entire skin in one go. They do this by rubbing against rough surfaces to loosen the old skin, then slithering out of it in one piece, revealing shiny new skin underneath.

☐ **4.** The tokay gecko has a surprising defense mechanism: it can make a loud barking noise. When threatened, this gecko will open its mouth wide and emit a distinctive "tokay" call, which can startle predators and give it a chance to escape.

☐ **5.** Reptiles are known for their long lifespans, but the Aldabra giant tortoise takes it to another level. These massive creatures can live for over 100 years, with some individuals reaching an astonishing age of 200 years or more.

☐ **6.** Chameleons are famous for their ability to change color, but did you know they do it to communicate, not to blend in with their surroundings? They use color changes to signal their mood, communicate with other chameleons, and regulate their body temperature.

☐ **7.** Some reptiles, like the New Zealand tuatara, have a third eye—well, sort of. Known as the parietal eye, it's a light-sensitive spot on top of the head that helps regulate their circadian rhythms and detect changes in light.

☐ **8.** The green anaconda is not only the heaviest snake in the world, but it's also one of the longest. These massive serpents can reach lengths of over 20 feet and weigh as much as 550 pounds.

☐ **9.** The green iguana has a secret weapon for escaping predators: it can detach its tail. When threatened, the iguana can break a weak spot in its tail, allowing it to escape while the predator is left with a wriggling distraction.

☐ **10.** The frilled lizard has a unique way of scaring off predators: it can unfurl a large frill of skin around its neck, making itself appear much larger and more intimidating. It's like having a built-in costume for Halloween every day.

☐ **11.** Crocodiles have a jaw-dropping bite force, but did you know they're also caring parents? Mother crocs carefully tend to their nests, protecting the eggs from predators and even gently rolling them in their mouths to help hatchlings emerge.

☐ **12.** Have you ever heard of a reptile that glows in the dark? The hawksbill sea turtle has fluorescent patterns on its shell that become visible under certain types of light. Common colors are orange, green, and red. It's like having a hidden superpower.

☐ **13.** Some reptiles have incredible camouflage abilities, like the leaf-tailed gecko. With its tail shaped and colored like a dead leaf, complete with veins and spots, it can blend seamlessly into its rainforest habitat, making it almost invisible to predators.

☐ **14.** While most lizards lay eggs, the blue-tongued skink gives birth to live young. These adorable babies emerge fully formed from their mother's body, ready to start exploring their environment.

☐ **15.** The Gila monster is one of the few venomous lizards in the world, and its bite can be quite painful. But did you know its venom could be the key to treating diabetes? Scientists are studying components of Gila monster venom for potential use in diabetes medications.

☐ **16.** Reptiles have some of the longest lifespans in the animal kingdom, and the Galápagos tortoise takes the prize for longevity. These ancient giants can live for well over 100 years, with some individuals surpassing the age of 150.

☐ **17.** The alligator snapping turtle is a master of deception. It lies in wait at the bottom of rivers and lakes, luring prey with its tongue, which looks like a worm. When unsuspecting fish swim in for a closer look, they become dinner.

☐ **18.** The horned lizard has a bizarre defense mechanism: it shoots blood from its eyes. When threatened, these unique reptiles can rupture blood vessels near their eyes, shooting a stream of blood up to 5 feet away, which can confuse and repel predators.

☐ **19.** Reptiles come in all shapes and sizes, but none are as peculiar as the mata mata turtle. With its flattened head and long, snorkel-like nose, it looks like something out of a prehistoric nightmare, but it's perfectly adapted for life in murky South American waters.

☐ **20.** The Komodo dragon is the largest lizard in the world, but its size isn't its only impressive feature. These apex predators also have a keen sense of smell, capable of detecting carrion from miles away, helping them locate their next meal.

☐ **21.** Unlike most lizards, which have smooth skin, the bearded dragon has specialized scales under its chin that puff out when it feels threatened, making it look like it has a beard. It's a clever trick to scare off potential predators!

☐ **22.** Snakes are famous for their ability to open their jaws to swallow prey much larger than their heads, but did you know they can have more than 300 bones (humans have 206 bones).

☐ **23.** The pancake tortoise might look flat as a pancake, but it's anything but flimsy. Its flattened shell allows it to squeeze into narrow crevices in rocky terrain, providing protection from predators and extreme temperatures.

☐ **24.** Some reptiles have mastered the art of playing dead to escape danger. The eastern hognose snake, for example, will flip onto its back and emit a foul odor to convince predators that it's not worth eating.

☐ **25.** The painted turtle can remarkably survive in icy conditions. When winter arrives and ponds freeze over, these resilient turtles can survive by entering a state called brumation (similar to hibernation), slowing down their metabolism to conserve energy until warmer weather returns.

# **Bonus**Facts

The tentacled snake has a truly remarkable hunting technique. It lies in wait at the bottom of rivers and lakes, waving its tentacle-like projections to mimic the movements of prey. When unsuspecting fish swim by, the snake strikes with lightning speed, snatching its meal.

Reptiles have a fascinating way of surviving harsh conditions. Some species, like the desert tortoise, can go for months without drinking water by storing it in their bladders and absorbing it slowly.

The gecko's incredible climbing ability comes from millions of tiny hairs on its feet called setae. These hairs create a molecular attraction known as van der Waals forces, allowing the gecko to stick to almost any surface, even upside down!

Some reptiles have evolved to survive in extreme environments, like the spiny-tailed lizard. Found in the deserts of Africa and Asia, this lizard can withstand temperatures exceeding 120°F by burrowing underground and regulating its body temperature.

# **Vocabulary**Builder

Carrion (*See No. 20*) is the decaying flesh of dead animals. It's a crucial food source for scavengers like vultures, crows, and insects. Despite its unpleasant nature, carrion serves an essential role in nature's cycle by recycling nutrients back into the ecosystem. As scavengers consume carrion, they prevent the spread of diseases that could arise from decaying carcasses. Ultimately, carrion contributes to maintaining a healthy and balanced ecosystem by supporting diverse animal populations.

# Chapter 4
# Ocean Friends

☐ **1.** The ocean is home to the vampire squid, which, despite its spooky name, doesn't suck blood but instead uses bioluminescence to create a glowing display when threatened.

☐ **2.** The oceans' deepest point is the Challenger Deep in the Mariana Trench, which plunges to a depth of over 36,000 feet. It's so deep that if Mount Everest were placed at the bottom, its peak would still be over a mile underwater.

☐ **3.** The oceans' deepest-dwelling fish, the hadal snailfish, lives at depths of over 26,000 feet in the Mariana Trench, enduring immense pressure and darkness.

☐ **4.** The peculiar-looking hammerhead shark's wide-set eyes give it a 360-degree view of its surroundings, aiding in hunting prey like stingrays and squid.

☐ **5.** Some fish, like the Japanese pufferfish, have intricate courtship rituals. Male pufferfish create stunning underwater "crop circles" on the ocean floor to attract females.

☐ **6.** The ocean sunfish, or mola mola, is one of the largest boney fish in the world. It often visits cleaning stations where small fish remove parasites from its skin, fins, and gills.

☐ **7.** The oceans' ecosystems are interconnected in surprising ways. For example, sea otters play a crucial role in maintaining kelp forests by preying on sea urchins, preventing them from overgrazing the kelp.

☐ **8.** The clownfish and the sea anemone share a remarkable relationship. The clownfish is immune to the sea anemone's sting, finding protection among its tentacles. In return, it cleans the anemone and scares away predators.

☐ **9.** The oceans' depths harbor mysterious creatures like the deep-sea anglerfish, which uses a bioluminescent lure to attract prey in the darkness where it resides.

☐ **10.** The manta ray, with its majestic wingspan, is a filter feeder, consuming large quantities of plankton as it glides gracefully through the water.

☐ **11.** Sea cucumbers have a bizarre defense mechanism. When threatened, they expel their internal organs, deterring predators with their sticky, toxin-filled guts while they regenerate their organs.

☐ **12.** The oceans' largest predator, the sperm whale, has the largest brain of any creature to have lived on Earth. Its brain weighs about 18 pounds and is highly developed, aiding in complex communication and navigation.

☐ **13.** The incredible intelligence of dolphins is well-known, but did you know they can also use tools? Dolphins in Shark Bay, Australia, use sponges to protect their noses while foraging on the seafloor, showing remarkable problem-solving skills.

☐ **14.** The oceans' coral reefs are bustling cities of biodiversity. Coral reefs cover less than 2 percent of the ocean floor but they support about 25 percent of all marine species, making them one of the most diverse ecosystems on the planet.

☐ **15.** The oceans' apex predator, the great white shark, has a bite force of up to 4,000 pounds per square inch, allowing it to easily crush the hard shells of sea turtles and other prey.

☐ **16.** The oceans' colossal inhabitants, like the blue whale, have astonishing feeding habits. An adult blue whale can consume nearly 4 tons of krill daily, using its baleen plates to filter-feed the tiny crustaceans.

☐ **17.** The gravitational pull of the sun and the moon influences the ocean's tides. During a spring tide, when the moon and sun align, the gravitational forces combine, creating higher high tides and lower low tides.

☐ **18.** The oceans' bioluminescent creatures, like the firefly squid, produce light through a chemical reaction called bioluminescence. This phenomenon helps them communicate, camouflage, and attract prey or mates in the dark depths.

☐ **19.** The oceans' inhabitants have evolved extraordinary adaptations for survival. The Antarctic toothfish, for example, has special proteins in its blood that act like antifreeze, allowing it to thrive in the frigid waters of the Southern Ocean.

☐ **20.** The oceans' deep-sea dwellers face extreme conditions, including high pressure and total darkness. Yet, creatures like the barreleye fish have developed unique features like transparent heads, allowing them to see above while staying hidden below.

☐ **21.** The oceans' coral reefs are not only beautiful but also essential for coastal protection. They act as natural barriers, reducing the impact of waves and storms, and safeguarding shorelines from erosion and flooding.

☐ **22.** The oceans' biodiversity extends to its smallest inhabitants. Zooplankton, tiny drifting animals, play a vital role in marine food webs, serving as the primary food source for many larger marine creatures.

☐ **23.** The oceans' fish have remarkable senses. Sharks, for instance, can detect the electrical fields produced by other creatures, helping them locate prey even when it's hidden from view.

☐ **24.** The oceans' currents play a crucial role in regulating Earth's climate. The Gulf Stream, for instance, transports warm water from the Gulf of Mexico to the North Atlantic, influencing weather patterns and climate in regions it passes through.

☐ **25.** The oceans' largest living structure is the Great Barrier Reef, stretching over 1,400 miles along the coast of Australia. It is so vast that it can be seen from space and harbors an incredible diversity of marine life.

# VocabularyBuilder

Bioluminescence (*See No. 1*) is a phenomenon in which organisms produce light through a chemical reaction within their bodies. This light emission occurs typically in marine creatures like jellyfish, fish, and certain types of plankton but can also be found in some insects and fungi. It serves various purposes, including communication, attracting prey or mates, and camouflage in the dark depths of the ocean.

# Chapter 5
# Incredible Insects

☐ **1.** The Hercules Beetle, found in Central and South America, is one of the strongest insects, able to objects up to 850 times its own weight.

☐ **2.** Honeybees communicate through intricate dances called "waggle dances" to tell others in the hive where to find food sources.

☐ **3.** The Malaysian Walking Leaf insect resembles a dead leaf, complete with veins and discoloration, making it nearly indistinguishable from a real leaf.

☐ **4.** Dragonflies are ancient insects; fossils suggest they've been around for over 300 million years, even before dinosaurs.

☐ **5.** The Brazilian treehopper has a bizarrely shaped pronotum that resembles a thorn or a leaf, providing camouflage and protection against predators.

☐ **6.** There's a species of moth called the "Hummingbird Hawk-Moth" that looks and moves like a tiny hummingbird, but it's actually a moth.

☐ **7.** The Bombardier Beetle has a unique defense mechanism: when threatened, it shoots hot, harmful chemicals from its abdomen, deterring predators.

☐ **8.** The orchid mantis resembles a flower petal, enabling it to blend into its surroundings to ambush prey, making it a master of camouflage.

☐ **9.** The Goliath Beetle, native to Africa, can grow to a length of 4.5 inches long and weigh as much as 3.5 ounces, making it one of the largest beetles in the world.

☐ **10.** Some species of termites build towering mounds that can be 20 feet tall or higher. These mounds are architectural marvels with sophisticated ventilation systems.

☐ **11.** Butterflies taste with their feet. Their taste receptors are on their feet, allowing them to determine if a plant is suitable for laying eggs.

☐ **12.** The Titan Beetle, found in South America, can grow up to 6.5 inches long, making it one of the largest insects on the planet.

☐ **13.** The diving bell spider is the only spider that spends nearly its entire life underwater, creating a bubble of air that it carries with it for breathing.

☐ **14.** Fireflies are not flies but are actually beetles. They use bioluminescence to attract mates, producing a magical glow on warm summer nights.

☐ **15.** There's a species of moth called the "Madagascan sunset moth" that displays a stunning array of colors and patterns, including iridescent colors on its wings.

☐ **16.** The praying mantis has excellent vision and can rotate its head 180 degrees to scan its surroundings for prey.

☐ **17.** Some species of ants "farm" aphids, protecting them from predators and "milking" them for honeydew, a sweet substance they produce.

☐ **18.** Ladybugs are considered lucky in many cultures. They're also voracious predators, capable of consuming hundreds of aphids in a single day.

☐ **19.** The Peanut-headed Lanternfly, known as the Fulcra laternaria, has a distinctive head that resembles a peanut shell, making it easily recognizable.

☐ **20.** Cockroaches can survive without their heads for weeks because they breathe through small holes in their bodies and have decentralized nervous systems.

☐ **21.** Some species of ants, like the trap-jaw ant, have jaws that snap shut at speeds of up to 145 miles per hour, allowing them to catch prey or defend the colony with incredible force.

☐ **22.** Insects such as bees and ants can recognize themselves in a mirror, showing a level of self-awareness previously thought to be exclusive to mammals and some birds.

☐ **23**. Estimates suggest there are between 6 million to 10 million insect species worldwide, making them the most diverse group of organisms on Earth. However, scientists believe many insect species remain undiscovered, particularly in tropical regions.

☐ **24.** Queen bees can lay up to 3,000 eggs in a single day, ensuring the continuity of their hive's population.

☐ **25.** Fleas may be tiny, but they are some of the best jumpers in the animal kingdom. They can leap distances up to 150 times their body length. To put that into perspective, it's like a human jumping the length of a football field.

# **Bonus**Facts

Many species of ants, like the leaf-cutter ants, form highly organized societies with specialized roles for different members, including workers, soldiers, and the queen.

The African driver ant forms massive raiding swarms that can consist of millions of individuals, devouring everything in their path, earning them the nickname "army ants."

The lanternfly nymphs produce a frothy substance called "honeydew" that attracts ants and other insects. The ants, in turn, protect the lanternflies from predators, forming a mutualistic relationship.

# **Vocabulary**Builder

The pronotum (*See No. 5*) is a protective plate-like structure found on the thorax of insects, covering the area between the head and the wings. It serves as armor, shielding the insect's delicate internal organs from harm. In some species the pronotum may be elaborately shaped or adorned to mimic features of the environment, providing camouflage against predators or enhancing the insect's ability to blend in with its surroundings.

# Chapter 6
# Fabulous Felines

☐ **1.** Cats have retractable claws, which means they can extend them when needed for hunting or climbing and retract them when not in use. This unique adaptation helps keep their claws sharp and prevents them from getting worn down while walking.

☐ **2.** A group of cats is called a "clowder." While most domestic cats are solitary creatures, they sometimes form social groups, especially in households with multiple cats.

☐ **3.** The smallest cat breed is the Singapura, originating from Singapore. They have large eyes and ears relative to their small size, making them incredibly adorable.

☐ **4.** The Norwegian Forest cat is a breed known for its thick, double-layered fur and tufted ears. It is well-adapted to cold climates and has a water-repellent coat that keeps it dry in rainy weather.

☐ **5.** Lions are the only cats that live in large groups called prides. These prides are typically made up of multiple related females and their offspring, along with a few adult males.

☐ **6.** The Cheetah is the fastest animal on land, reaching speeds up to 75 miles per hour in short bursts. Its slender, aerodynamic build and long, muscular legs contribute to its incredible speed.

☐ **7.** Domestic cats have five toes on their front paws and four toes on their back paws. However, some cats may have extra toes due to a genetic condition called polydactylism, which is more common in certain breeds like the Maine Coon.

☐ **8.** The Maine Coon is one of the largest domestic cat breeds, known for its friendly disposition and tufted ears. Despite their size, they are gentle and often called "gentle giants."

☐ **9.** The Manx cat is unique in that it is born without a tail or a very short tail due to a genetic mutation characteristic of the breed.

☐ **10.** Cats have a special scent gland located on their forehead, called the "supraorbital gland," which they use to mark their territory by rubbing their head against objects.

☐ **11.** Tigers have striped skin, not just striped fur. If you were to remove a tiger's fur, you would see its distinctive stripe pattern on its skin.

☐ **12.** Black panthers are not a separate species but rather melanistic variants of leopards and jaguars. This genetic mutation causes an excess of melanin, resulting in a black coat.

☐ **13.** A tiger's roar can be heard up to 2 miles away. This powerful vocalization serves to establish territory and communicate with other tigers.

☐ **14.** The Margay, a small wild cat native to Central and South America, is an excellent tree climber. Its flexible ankles allow it to climb down trees headfirst, like a squirrel.

☐ **15.** Ocelots, a wild cat species in the Americas, have distinctive spots and stripes on their fur, making them excellent camouflagers in their forest habitats.

☐ **16.** The Scottish Fold is a domestic cat breed known for its unique folded ears, which give it an adorable and distinctive appearance.

☐ **17.** The Turkish Van is a breed of domestic cat known for its love of water. Unlike most cats, they enjoy swimming and playing in bodies of water.

☐ **18.** Servals, native to Africa, have the longest legs relative to body size of all cat species. These long legs help them navigate through tall grass as they hunt for prey.

☐ **19.** Caracals, also known as desert lynx, have tufted ears similar to those of the lynx but are not closely related. They are skilled hunters, capable of taking down birds in mid-flight.

☐ **20.** The Fishing Cat, native to Southeast Asia, is a good swimmer, which helps it hunt fish, frogs, and other aquatic prey. Its partially webbed feet make it well-suited for life in and around water.

☐ **21.** Jaguars have the strongest bite force of any big cat relative to their size. With their powerful jaws, they can easily crush the bones and shells of their prey.

☐ **22.** The Pallas's cat is a small wild cat native to Central Asia. It has a distinctive, flat face with expressive eyes, giving it a somewhat grumpy appearance.

☐ **23.** The Sand Cat is a small wild cat found in deserts across North Africa and Southwest Asia. Its thick fur on its paws provides insulation from the hot sand and allows it to walk comfortably on scorching surfaces.

☐ **24.** The Sphynx cat is a hairless breed known for its wrinkled skin and large ears. Despite its lack of fur, it is not entirely hypoallergenic and still produces dander.

☐ **25.** The Bengal cat is a domestic breed known for its distinctive spotted or marbled coat, reminiscent of its wild ancestor, the Asian leopard cat.

# **Bonus**Facts

The Siamese cat is one of the oldest and most recognizable domestic cat breeds, known for its striking blue eyes and vocal nature.

The Bobcat is a North American wild cat with distinctive tufted ears and a short, bobbed tail. It is an adaptable predator found in a variety of habitats, from forests to deserts.

The "King of the Jungle" moniker for lions is a bit of a misnomer since lions primarily inhabit grasslands and savannas, not jungles. However, they are indeed apex predators in their habitats.

# **Vocabulary**Builder

Melanistic Variant (*See No. 12*) refers to a genetic condition where an animal produces an excess of melanin pigment, resulting in a darker-than-usual appearance. In the context of cats, melanistic variants occur in species like leopards and jaguars, producing individuals with black coats instead of the typical spotted or rosetted patterns. Despite their dark appearance, these animals retain the same species characteristics and behaviors as their non-melanistic counterparts.

# Chapter 7
# Curious About Canines

☐ **1.** African wild dogs, also called painted wolves, operate on a democratic system when making group decisions, such as when to hunt or rest. The pack will gather and "vote" by sneezing, with more sneezes indicating a stronger consensus.

☐ **2.** In the chilling landscapes of the Arctic, sled dogs like Siberian Huskies and Alaskan Malamutes showcase incredible endurance. They can run over 100 miles in a single day, pulling heavy sleds through snow and ice.

☐ **3.** Dingoes, wild dogs native to Australia, exhibit fascinating parenting behaviors. The responsibility of raising the pups is shared by both parents. This cooperative parenting helps ensure the pups' survival in the harsh Australian outback, where resources can be scarce.

☐ **4.** Dachshunds, with their long bodies and short legs, were originally bred in Germany to hunt badgers. Their elongated shape and fearlessness allowed them to burrow into badger dens to flush out their prey.

☐ **5.** The Tibetan Mastiff holds the record for the world's most expensive dog, with one pup reportedly sold for over $1.5 million These majestic giants are prized by collectors and dog enthusiasts alike.

☐ **6.** The Basenji is often called the "barkless dog" because it doesn't bark. Instead, it produces a unique sound described as a yodel or a baroo, which it uses to communicate.

☐ **7.** The Chow Chow is famous for its distinctive blue-black tongue, a trait shared by only a few other breeds. Despite various theories, the origin of this unique feature remains a mystery.

☐ **8.** The Greyhound is the fastest dog breed and is able to reach speeds up to 45 miles per hour in short bursts. Their slender build, powerful muscles, and aerodynamic design make them the ultimate sprinters.

☐ **9.** Small but mighty, the swift fox is the smallest wild canid in North America. Despite its diminutive size, it's a speedy sprinter and is able to reach speeds up to 40 miles per hour.

☐ **10.** The Pekingese breed has a regal history, going back more than 2,000 years to ancient China. Bred to resemble lions, they were favored by Chinese royalty and nobility as companions and palace guardians.

☐ **11.** Basset Hounds possess an exceptional sense of smell, second only to the Bloodhound. Their keen olfactory abilities make them valuable assets in tracking and scent detection tasks, earning them a reputation as skilled hunters and search-and-rescue dogs.

☐ **12.** Labrador Retrievers have been one of the most popular dog breeds in the United States for more than 30 years. They are known for their intelligence, versatility, and friendly disposition.

☐ **13.** Also known as the Xoloitzcuintli or simply Xolo, the Mexican Hairless Dog is prized for its hairlessness, making it an ideal companion in warm climates. Interestingly, their lack of fur means they have higher body temperatures than most dogs, giving them a warm and soothing touch.

☐ **14.** The Cavalier King Charles Spaniel is named after King Charles II of England, who favored these charming little dogs. They were often depicted in royal portraits alongside the king.

☐ **15.** Dholes, also known as Asiatic wild dogs, live in tight-knit clans usually consisting of approximately 15 individuals although it can sometimes be as high as 40 individuals.

☐ **16.** Jackals are highly vocal animals, communicating with a diverse range of sounds, including barks, howls, yaps, and growls. Each vocalization serves a specific purpose, from territorial displays to coordinating hunts.

☐ **17.** Just as humans have unique fingerprints, dogs have individual nose prints that can be used for identification. The pattern of ridges and creases on a dog's nose is as distinct as a human fingerprint and can be used to positively identify lost or stolen dogs.

☐ **18.** Gray wolves possess an extraordinary sense of smell, capable of detecting scents from up to 1.75 miles away. This keen olfactory ability helps them locate prey, communicate with pack members over long distances, and navigate their expansive territories. Their sense of smell is estimated to be 100,000 times more sensitive than that of humans, making them formidable hunters in the wild.

☐ **19.** Like humans, dogs experience rapid eye movement (REM) sleep, which is associated with dreaming. Studies have shown that dogs exhibit brain patterns similar to the brain patterns of humans during REM sleep, suggesting that they indeed dream. You might see your dog twitching, whimpering, or even "running" in their sleep, indicating that they're engaged in a dreamworld of their own.

☐ **20.** The Puli breed is famous for its distinctive corded coat, which forms naturally into long, cord-like dreadlocks. These cords serve as protection against harsh weather and predators in their native Hungary while also giving them a unique and striking appearance that sets them apart from other breeds.

☐ **21.** Coyotes are skilled vocal mimics capable of imitating the sounds of other animals like birds, rabbits, and even domestic dogs. This ability allows them to deceive potential prey or rivals, luring them into vulnerable positions or intimidating them with false alarm calls.

☐ **22.** Dalmatians have a long history as firehouse mascots, dating back to the days of horse-drawn fire carriages. Their agility and endurance made them valuable assets in guiding and protecting horses, while their distinctive spotted coats helped them stand out in the chaos of firefighting scenes.

☐ **23.** Despite its name, the maned wolf is not a wolf or a fox. It's the largest canid in South America and belongs to a unique genus. With its long legs and fox-like features, the maned wolf is a striking example of convergent evolution, adapting to its grassland habitat in a distinct and fascinating way.

□ **24.** Doberman Pinschers are known for their versatility and intelligence. They excel in various roles, including police work, search and rescue, therapy, and competitive sports like obedience and agility. Their athleticism, loyalty, and keen intellect make them valuable partners in a wide range of activities.

□ **25.** The howler monkey isn't the only creature with a powerful voice. The gray wolf's howl can be heard up to 10 miles away, making it one of the loudest animal calls in the world. This distinctive sound isn't just for communication; it also helps wolves locate each other in dense forests and across vast distances.

# **Bonus**Facts

The Great Dane holds the record for the world's tallest dog breed. Originating from Germany, these gentle giants can tower over humans when they stand on their hind legs. Despite their imposing size, Great Danes are known for their friendly and affectionate nature, often referred to as "gentle giants."

The Yorkshire Terrier, or "Yorkie," may be small in stature but boasts a glamorous history. Originally bred in 19th-century England to catch rats in textile mills, they later became fashionable companions for Victorian-era ladies. Their long, silky coats were often styled in elaborate hairstyles, earning them the nickname "the fashion model of the dog world."

The Saluki, an ancient breed originating from the Middle East, holds the distinction of being one of the oldest known domesticated dog breeds. Revered for their grace, speed, and loyalty, Salukis have been depicted in ancient Egyptian tombs, dating back over 4,000 years.

# **Vocabulary**Builder

Canid (*See No. 9*) refers to any member of the biological family Canidae, which encompasses a diverse group of carnivorous mammals commonly known as canines or simply "dogs." This family includes domesticated dogs, as well as their wild relatives such as wolves, foxes, coyotes, jackals, and other similar species. Canids share common characteristics such as a keen sense of smell, sharp teeth, and a carnivorous diet, making them well-adapted predators across a variety of habitats worldwide.

# Chapter 8
# American History

☐ **1.** Gilbert Stuart's portrait of George Washington, painted in 1796, became the basis for the image on the one-dollar bill and is considered the first official presidential portrait.

☐ **2.** Established in 1872, Yellowstone National Park is the world's first national park, known for its stunning geysers, hot springs, and diverse wildlife.

☐ **3.** The California Gold Rush of 1848-1855 drew thousands of fortune seekers to California after gold was discovered at Sutter's Mill, sparking rapid population growth and economic development in the region.

☐ **4.** On December 17, 1903, Orville and Wilbur Wright achieved the first powered, controlled flight at Kitty Hawk, North Carolina, marking a significant milestone in aviation history.

☐ **5.** President Abraham Lincoln issued the Emancipation Proclamation on January 1, 1863, declaring all enslaved people in Confederate-held territory to be forever free, a crucial step toward abolishing slavery in the United States.

☐ **6.** In 1869, Wyoming became the first territory to grant women the right to vote, paving the way for women's suffrage movements across the country.

☐ **7.** Completed on May 10, 1869, the Transcontinental Railroad connected the West Coast and East Coast of the United States, revolutionizing transportation and trade across the country.

☐ **8.** The Statue of Liberty, a gift from France, was dedicated on October 28, 1886. It serves as a symbol of freedom and democracy, welcoming immigrants arriving in New York Harbor.

☐ **9.** The devastating fire of October 8-10, 1871, destroyed much of Chicago, leading to widespread rebuilding efforts and advancements in fire safety regulations and urban planning.

☐ **10.** The Battle of the Alamo, fought from February 23 to March 6, 1836, was a crucial event in the Texas Revolution. A small force bravely defended the Alamo mission against Mexican troops, inspiring future generations with their courage and sacrifice.

☐ **11.** On July 20, 1969, Apollo 11 astronauts Neil Armstrong and Buzz Aldrin became the first people to walk on the moon, with Armstrong's famous words, "That's one small step for [a] man, one giant leap for mankind."

☐ **12.** In 1803, the United States purchased the Louisiana Territory from France for $15 million, doubling the size of the country and opening up vast new lands for settlement and exploration.

☐ **13.** From the 1830s to the 1860s, over 400,000 pioneers traveled the Oregon Trail from Missouri to Oregon, enduring hardships and challenges in search of a better life in the West.

☐ **14.** Adopted on July 4, 1776, the Declaration of Independence proclaimed the American colonies' separation from British rule, laying the foundation for the formation of the United States of America.

☐ **15.** The stock market crash of 1929 marked the start of the Great Depression, a decade-long economic downturn that left millions of Americans unemployed and struggling to make ends meet.

☐ **16.** The Civil Rights Movement of the 1950s and 1960s fought against discrimination and racial segregation, culminating in landmark legislation like the Civil Rights Act of 1964 and the Voting Rights Act of 1965.

☐ **17.** In the 1930s, severe drought and poor farming practices led to the Dust Bowl, a period of massive dust storms that devastated the Great Plains, forcing many farmers to abandon their land and migrate westward in search of work.

☐ **18.** Completed in 1936, the Hoover Dam, located on the border between Arizona and Nevada, is one of the largest concrete structures in the world. It provides hydroelectric power and controls the flow of the Colorado River.

☐ **19.** A network of secret routes and safe houses, the Underground Railroad helped enslaved African Americans escape to the northern states and Canada in the years leading up to the Civil War.

☐ **20.** Fought from July 1 to July 3, 1863, the Battle of Gettysburg was pivotal in the Civil War. Union forces repelled Confederate advances and secured a crucial victory that shifted the conflict's momentum.

☐ **21.** The Women's Suffrage Movement fought for women's right to vote and culminated in the ratification of the 19th Amendment in 1920 which granted women suffrage nationwide.

☐ **22.** Completed in 1825, the Erie Canal connected the Hudson River to the Great Lakes, allowing for cheaper and faster transportation of goods and people between the Midwest and the East Coast, spurring economic growth and development.

☐ **23.** In the 1920s and 1930s, Harlem, New York City, became the center of a cultural movement known as the Harlem Renaissance, celebrating African American art, music, literature, and intellectualism.

☐ **24.** In October 1962, the United States and the Soviet Union found themselves on the brink of nuclear war during the Cuban Missile Crisis, a 13-day standoff over the presence of Soviet missiles in Cuba, ultimately resolved through diplomacy and negotiation.

☐ **25.** Completed in 1861, the Transcontinental Telegraph connected the East and West coasts of the United States for the first time, revolutionizing communication and reducing the time it took to send messages from weeks to minutes.

# **Vocabulary**Builder

Suffrage (*See No. 6*) refers to the right to vote in political elections, particularly in the context of women's suffrage. Historically, women's suffrage was a movement advocating for women to be granted this fundamental democratic right, which was often denied to them based on gender. Achieving women's suffrage required extensive activism, protests, and legislative efforts, ultimately resulting in the granting of voting rights to women in various countries around the world.

# Chapter 9
# Founding Fathers

☐ **1.** On July 4, 1776, fifty-six delegates from the 13 American Colonies signed the Declaration of Independence. This pivotal document, authored primarily by Thomas Jefferson, declared the colonies' independence from British rule and asserted the inherent rights of all people to life, liberty, and the pursuit of happiness.

☐ **2.** The youngest person to sign the Declaration of Independence was Edward Rutledge of South Carolina, who was just 26 years old at the time of signing. Despite his youth, Rutledge played a significant role in the independence movement.

☐ **3.** Benjamin Franklin, at the age of 70, was the oldest person to sign the Declaration of Independence. His vast experience as a scientist, inventor, and diplomat made him a crucial figure in the American Revolution.

☐ **4.** Thomas Jefferson, the principal author of the Declaration of Independence, spoke six languages and could read two others.

☐ **5.** George Washington, the first U.S. president, had a set of false teeth made from human teeth and hippopotamus ivory.

☐ **6.** Alexander Hamilton, one of the Founding Fathers, founded the Bank of New York in 1784, making it the oldest bank in the United States.

☐ **7.** John Adams and Thomas Jefferson, both signers of the Declaration of Independence and later presidents, died on the same day—July 4, 1826, exactly fifty years after the adoption of the Declaration.

☐ **8.** James Madison, often called the "Father of the Constitution," was the shortest U.S. president, standing just 5 feet 4 inches tall.

☐ **9.** John Hancock, known for his prominent signature on the Declaration of Independence, reportedly signed it with such large letters so that King George III could read it without his glasses.

☐ **10.** Richard Henry Lee, known for introducing the resolution for independence to the Continental Congress in 1776, was also a signatory of the Articles of Confederation.

☐ **11.** George Washington, in addition to being a military leader and statesman, was an avid farmer and experimented with various agricultural techniques on his estate at Mount Vernon.

☐ **12.** John Jay, one of the authors of the Federalist Papers, later became the first Chief Justice of the United States Supreme Court, shaping the early development of American jurisprudence.

☐ **13.** The 21st Amendment, ratified in 1933, repealed Prohibition, the 18th Amendment's ban on alcohol. It returned the authority to regulate alcohol to the states, marking the end of a failed social experiment.

☐ **14.** The Bill of Rights was added to the Constitution in 1791 to address concerns about individual liberties and rights.

☐ **15.** Roger Sherman, a Founding Father from Connecticut, proposed the Great Compromise at the Constitutional Convention, which resolved the dispute between large and small states over representation in Congress.

☐ **16.** The Constitution outlines the structure of the federal government and its three branches: the legislative, executive, and judicial branches.

☐ **17.** Patrick Henry, known for his stirring speeches advocating for American independence, famously declared, "Give me liberty, or give me death!" during a speech in 1775.

☐ **18.** The 27th Amendment, which pertains to congressional pay raises, was originally proposed in 1789 but not ratified until 1992, making it the most recently adopted amendment. It stipulates that any change in the compensation of members of Congress cannot take effect until after the next election of the House of Representatives.

☐ **19.** George Mason, a delegate to the Constitutional Convention, refused to sign the final draft of the United States Constitution because it did not include a bill of rights advocating for individual liberties and protections.

☐ **20.** The U.S. Constitution has been amended 27 times since its ratification in 1787.

☐ **21.** The original Declaration of Independence is kept in the National Archives in Washington, D.C., but it wasn't always there. During the Revolutionary War, it was moved around to keep it safe from British troops.

☐ **22.** The Constitution begins with the famous words, "We the People," emphasizing the document's focus on the power and authority of the American people.

☐ **23.** Elbridge Gerry, a signer of the Declaration of Independence, is known for giving his name to the term "gerrymandering," a practice of manipulating electoral district boundaries for political advantage.

☐ **24.** Rufus King, a delegate to the Constitutional Convention and a signer of the United States Constitution, later served as a United States Senator and diplomat.

☐ **25.** Gouverneur Morris, a delegate to the Constitutional Convention, is credited with penning much of the final draft of the United States Constitution, including its famous preamble.

# **Bonus**Facts

The Constitution was signed by 39 delegates at the Constitutional Convention in Philadelphia in 1787.

The Declaration of Independence was first read to the public on July 8, 1776, in Philadelphia's Independence Square.

# **Vocabulary**Builder

Jurisprudence (*See No. 12*) is the study and understanding of law. It explores how laws are made, interpreted, and applied in society. Jurisprudence examines legal principles, theories, and systems to understand the reasoning behind laws and their effects on individuals and communities. It helps shape legal decisions and the development of legal systems.

# Chapter 10
# Monumental Monuments

☐ **1.** The USS Arizona Memorial in Pearl Harbor, Hawaii, straddles the sunken hull of the battleship USS Arizona, which was sunk during the surprise attack on Pearl Harbor on December 7, 1941, marking the entry of the United States into World War II.

☐ **2.** The Eiffel Tower in Paris, France, grows in height during the summer due to the expansion of its iron structure in the heat.

☐ **3.** The Vietnam Veterans Memorial in Washington, D.C., features 58,318 names engraved on black granite walls, honoring those who died or went missing during the Vietnam War.

☐ **4.** The Lincoln Memorial's statue of Lincoln is 19 feet tall and made of 28 blocks of Georgia marble.

☐ **5.** The Statue of Liberty in New York City was originally intended to be a lighthouse. It was a gift from France to the United States in 1886.

☐ **6.** The Iwo Jima Memorial in Arlington, Virginia, depicts Marines raising the U.S. Flag on Mount Suribachi during the battle of Iwo Jima in War II, commemorating the sacrifices of the U.S. Marine Corps in the Pacific theater.

☐ **7.** The National World War II Memorial in Washington, D.C., features 56 granite pillars representing U.S. states and territories, as well as a wall of 4,048 gold stars. Each star represents 100 Americans who died in the war.

☐ **8.** The Washington Monument's height was limited to 555 feet 5 inches due to a lack of funds and the possibility of damaging the foundations of nearby buildings.

☐ **9.** Mount Rushmore in South Dakota, features the faces of four U.S. presidents carved into the granite cliffside: George Washington, Thomas Jefferson, Theodore Roosevelt, and Abraham Lincoln.

☐ **10.** The 9/11 Memorial & Museum in New York City honors the nearly 3,000 victims of the September 11, 2001, terrorist attacks. It features a pair of reflecting pools in the footprint of the Twin Towers and a museum displaying artifacts and stories of survival and remembrance.

☐ **11.** Stonehenge in England is over 4,000 years old, and its exact purpose—whether ceremonial, astronomical, or religious—remains a mystery.

☐ **12.** The Christ the Redeemer statue in Rio de Janeiro, Brazil, stands atop Corcovado Mountain and overlooks the city, symbolizing peace and welcoming visitors.

☐ **13.** The Rapa Nui people carved the Moai statues on Easter Island, Chile, between 1400 and 1650 AD. However, the methods used to transport them across the island remain uncertain.

☐ **14.** The Pyramids of Giza in Egypt are over 4,500 years old and were built as tombs for pharaohs. The Great Pyramid is considered one of the Seven Wonders of the Ancient World.

☐ **15.** The Leaning Tower of Pisa in Italy leans due to an unstable foundation and has been tilting since its construction began in 1173.

☐ **16.** The Sydney Opera House, a UNESCO World Heritage Site in Australia, has over 1 million roof tiles covering its sail-like structures.

☐ **17.** The Liberty Memorial in Kansas City, Missouri, was dedicated in 1926 as a memorial to the soldiers who fought and died in World War I. It features the iconic "Guardian of the Memory" statue and the National World War I Museum.

☐ **18.** The Soldiers and Sailors Monument in Indianapolis, Indiana, is a neoclassical monument dedicated to Indiana's veterans of the wars prior to World War I. It stands 284 feet tall and features bronze statues representing the Army, Navy, Artillery, and Cavalry.

☐ **19.** The United States Air Force Memorial in Arlington, Virginia, features three stainless steel spires soaring into the sky, representing the Air Force's core values: integrity first, service before self, and excellence in all we do.

☐ **20.** The National Memorial Arch in Valley Forge, Pennsylvania, commemorates the perseverance and sacrifice of George Washington's Continental Army during the harsh winter of 1777-1778 at Valley Forge.

☐ **21.** The Parthenon in Athens, Greece, was dedicated to the goddess Athena and is one of the most outstanding achievements of ancient Greek architecture.

☐ **22.** The Gettysburg National Cemetery in Gettysburg, Pennsylvania, is the final resting place for more than 3,500 Union soldiers who died during the Battle of Gettysburg in the American Civil War. It also houses a monument honoring President Abraham Lincoln's Gettysburg Address.

☐ **23.** The Alhambra in Granada, Spain, is a stunning example of Moorish architecture and was originally built as a fortress in the 9th century.

☐ **24.** The Burj Khalifa in Dubai, UAE, is the tallest building in the world. At over 2,700 feet, it features an observation deck offering breathtaking views.

☐ **25.** The Acropolis of Athens, Greece, is a hilltop citadel featuring several ancient buildings, including the iconic Parthenon, dedicated to the goddess Athena.

# **Bonus**Facts

The Hagia Sophia in Istanbul, Turkey, has served as a church, mosque, and museum over its long history. Its architecture blends elements of Byzantine and Ottoman architecture.

The Sistine Chapel in Vatican City is famous for its stunning frescoes, including Michelangelo's masterpiece on the ceiling depicting scenes from Genesis.

# **Vocabulary**Builder

A UNESCO World Heritage Site (*See No. 16*) is a place of special cultural or natural significance that is protected by the United Nations Educational, Scientific and Cultural Organization (UNESCO). These sites are recognized for their outstanding universal value and are preserved for future generations to appreciate and enjoy.

# Chapter 11
# American Treasures

☐ **1.** The White House has 132 rooms, including 35 bathrooms, 28 fireplaces, and 3 elevators. Its Oval Office has been the workplace of every U.S. president since President Taft in 1909.

☐ **2.** The Golden Gate Bridge's iconic color, "International Orange," was chosen for its visibility in the bay's foggy conditions. Its main cables contain enough wire to encircle the Earth over three times.

☐ **3.** The Grand Canyon is so vast that it can fit the entire city of New York within its boundaries.

☐ **4.** The Liberty Bell in Philadelphia, Pennsylvania, weighs over 2,000 pounds and was originally cast in 1752 in England.

☐ **5.** The Great Smoky Mountains National Park is one of the few places in the world where synchronous fireflies can be seen, lighting up the night with their synchronized flashes.

☐ **6.** The Brooklyn Bridge, opened in 1883, was the first steel-wire suspension bridge ever built.

☐ **7.** The National Mall in Washington, D.C., has iconic monuments and memorials, including the Washington Monument, Lincoln Memorial, and Vietnam Veterans Memorial.

☐ **8.** When completed in 1931, the Empire State Building was the world's tallest building, standing at 1,454 feet tall. Its construction used over 10 million bricks and 730 tons of aluminum and stainless steel.

☐ **9.** The White House has been the residence of every U.S. president since John Adams in 1800. Its Truman Balcony was added in 1947 by President Truman as a private balcony for the first family.

☐ **10.** Mount Rushmore's construction took 14 years to complete, from 1927 to 1941.

☐ **11**. The Statue of Liberty's copper exterior is the thickness of two pennies and has developed its green patina over time. Its crown has 25 windows, symbolizing gemstones and the heaven's rays.

☐ **12**. The Brooklyn Bridge's construction used over 600 workers and took 14 years to complete.

☐ **13**. The Lincoln Memorial was dedicated by President Warren G. Harding on May 30, 1922, in a ceremony attended by thousands of people.

☐ **14**. Sequoia National Park's Giant Forest is home to groves of giant sequoia trees, including the General Sherman Tree, which is estimated to be more than 2,000 years old.

☐ **15**. The Great Smoky Mountains National Park is more than 522,000 acres and spans two states—Tennessee and North Carolina—and is the most biologically diverse National Park.

☐ **16**. The National Mall's Reflecting Pool stretches over 2,000 feet and is flanked by the Lincoln Memorial and the Washington Monument.

☐ **17**. Death Valley National Park in California is the lowest, hottest, and driest national park in the United States, with temperatures reaching over 130°F.

☐ **18**. Arches National Park in Utah contains over 2,000 natural sandstone arches, including the iconic Delicate Arch.

☐ **19**. Grant Wood's painting "American Gothic" features a farmer and his daughter posing in front of a house in Eldon, Iowa, which still stands today as a tourist attraction.

☐ **20**. Norman Rockwell's painting "Freedom from Want" is one of four iconic images representing the Four Freedoms discussed by President Franklin D. Roosevelt in a speech in 1941.

☐ **21.** "American Progress" by John Gast is an allegorical painting that depicts Manifest Destiny, with a woman representing "Progress" carrying a schoolbook and telegraph wire while settlers and a train move westward.

☐ **22.** In 2014. Georgia O'Keeffe's painting "Jimson Weed/White Flower No. 1" sold for $44.4 million, setting a record for the highest price ever paid for a painting by a female artist.

☐ **23.** Established in 1872, Yellowstone National Park is America's first national park and is home to the Old Faithful geyser, which erupts roughly every 90 minutes.

☐ **24.** Yosemite National Park's Half Dome is a popular hiking destination, with a 400-foot cable route leading to its summit.

☐ **25.** Everglades National Park, the largest tropical wilderness in the U.S., is often called the "River of Grass."

# **Bonus**Facts

The Declaration of Independence is stored in a bulletproof glass case filled with argon gas to preserve it.

The Statue of Liberty's original torch was replaced in 1986 and is now displayed in the museum inside the pedestal.

Denali National Park, home to North America's tallest peak, Mount McKinley, was established in 1917 as Mount McKinley National Park.

# **Vocabulary**Builder

Allegorical (*See No. 21*) refers to a way of expressing ideas or telling stories through symbols or metaphors. In allegorical works, characters, events, or objects represent abstract concepts or moral qualities. This allows the author or artist to convey deeper meanings beyond the literal interpretation, often addressing universal themes or moral lessons.

# Chapter 12
# Matters Of Money

☐ **1.** The highest U.S. denomination ever printed was the $100,000 bill featuring President Woodrow Wilson. It was issued from 1934 to 1935 and used only for transactions between Federal Reserve Banks. It was never circulated among the public.

☐ **2.** The first U.S. coins were minted in 1793, with the Flowing Hair Liberty design on the copper cent and the half-cent.

☐ **3.** The 1933 Double Eagle $20 gold coin holds the record for the highest price ever paid for a coin at auction, fetching almost $19 million in 2021.

☐ **4.** The U.S. introduced a series of dollar coins featuring prominent figures like Susan B. Anthony, Sacagawea, and Presidents, but they haven't gained widespread circulation.

☐ **5.** Some bills with mismatched serial numbers, known as "mules," are considered valuable by collectors due to their rarity.

☐ **6.** U.S. currency incorporates advanced security features, including microprinting, color-shifting ink, and intricate watermarks, to deter counterfeiters.

☐ **7.** During World War II, special bills known as "Hawaii Overprint" Notes were issued for use in Hawaii with the word "Hawaii" overprinted on them to prevent enemy forces from using captured currency.

☐ **8.** The $2 bill is considered rare by some, but it's still in circulation. Its scarcity is often attributed to misconceptions, not actual rarity.

☐ **9.** The faces on U.S. bills weren't always presidents. Alexander Hamilton graced the $10 bill while Salmon P. Chase, Secretary of the Treasury, appeared on the $10,000 bill.

☐ **10.** U.S. currency features hidden symbols and messages. Some people say there is an owl (or spider) in the upper right corner of the one-dollar bill, which some believe to be linked to secret societies.

☐ **11.** "In God We Trust" first appeared on U.S. coins during the Civil War, but it became mandatory on all currency in 1955, reflecting a national sentiment during the Cold War.

☐ **12.** The Eye of Providence, often associated with divine providence, appears on the reverse of the one-dollar bill above the pyramid.

☐ **13.** During the Civil War, the U.S. government issued fractional currency in denominations less than one dollar to address a shortage of coins.

☐ **14.** The U.S. Secret Service, initially established to combat counterfeit currency, now primarily focuses on protecting current and former national leaders.

☐ **15.** U.S. paper currency earned the nickname "greenback" during the Civil War due to its distinctive green ink on the reverse side.

☐ **16.** Periodically, the U.S. faces coin shortages, leading to initiatives like the "Change Matters" campaign to encourage the circulation of spare change.

☐ **17.** The portraits on U.S. currency are engraved by master engravers, requiring precision and skill to capture the likeness of historical figures.

☐ **18.** The "Gold Coin" Certificates—These bills, issued in the late 19th and early 20th centuries, were redeemable for gold coins of equivalent value and helped facilitate transactions during times of economic uncertainty.

☐ **19.** The "Silver Certificates" bills were once redeemable for silver dollars but were phased out in the 1960s as the U.S. moved away from the gold and silver standards.

☐ **20.** The "Interest Bearing" Notes—These bills, issued during the Civil War, were the first to bear interest and were used to fund the Union war effort.

☐ **21.** Occasionally, printing errors result in unique and valuable bills, like the "double-denomination" notes where one side is printed with a different denomination.

☐ **22.** The "Black Eagle" large-size bills from the 1899 series feature a striking eagle on the front and were used primarily for transactions between Federal Reserve Banks.

☐ **23.** The "Educational Series," issued in 1896, featured intricate designs symbolizing science, industry, and education, reflecting the country's progress at the time.

☐ **24.** The "Demand Notes"—These bills, issued in the early 1860s, were the first paper currency issued by the U.S. government and were redeemable in coin on demand.

☐ **25.** The "National Gold Bank" Notes issued by certain banks in the 1870s were backed by gold deposits and could be redeemed for gold coins.

# **Bonus**Facts

The "Martha Washington" Silver Certificates, issued in the late 19th and early 20th centuries, featured a portrait of Martha Washington, making her the first woman to appear on U.S. currency.

The "Rainbow Series" bills, issued in 1869, were the first to feature vibrant colors, enhancing their aesthetic appeal and making them popular among collectors.

The "Bison" Notes—These large-size bills from the 1901 series feature an image of a bison on the front and were used primarily for transactions between Federal Reserve Banks.

The "Legal Tender" Notes—These bills, issued in the mid-19th century, were the first to be designated as "legal tender" by the U.S. government, meaning they could be used to pay debts.

# **Vocabulary**Builder

In the context of money, denomination (*See No. 1*) refers to the face value or monetary worth assigned to a specific unit of currency, such as a coin or banknote. Different denominations allow for convenient transactions by providing a range of values, from small amounts for everyday purchases to larger sums for significant transactions.

# Chapter 13
# Uniquely Human

☐ **1.** Robert Wadlow, the tallest person in recorded history, stood at a staggering 8 feet 11 inches tall. Nicknamed the "Alton Giant," he reached this remarkable height due to an overactive pituitary gland.

☐ **2.** Jyoti Amge from India holds the Guinness World Record for being the world's smallest woman. Standing at just 2 feet 0.7 inches tall, she has achondroplasia, a form of dwarfism.

☐ **3.** Your body has a superhighway of blood vessels totaling about 60,000 miles. That's like traveling around Earth's equator more than twice.

☐ **4.** Did you know you have 206 bones in your body? Your skull has 22 of them. The smallest bone, the stapes, is in your ear, measuring just 0.1 inches. The longest bone, the femur (thigh bone), is about 1/4 of your height.

☐ **5.** Jon Brower Minnoch, from the United States, is the heaviest person ever recorded. At his peak, he weighed a jaw-dropping 1,400 pounds due to several factors, including severe obesity and metabolic issues.

☐ **6.** Your digestive system is a busy factory. It's about 30 feet long and processes food in 24 to 72 hours.

☐ **7.** Your body is home to over 600 muscles, each with a unique job. In proportion to its size, the strongest muscle is the masseter in your jaw. Pound for pound, it's stronger than any other muscle.

☐ **8.** Your heart pumps about 2,000 gallons of blood through your blood vessels daily, delivering oxygen and nutrients to your cells.

☐ **9.** Your skin is amazing. It's your largest organ and weighs about 6 pounds. But did you know it's also sensitive? Your fingertips have about 2,500 touch receptors per square centimeter, helping you feel the world around you.

☐ **10.** Your brain is the boss. It's the most complex organ, with over 86 billion neurons. But it's not the heaviest; it's about 2 percent of your body weight. Still, it uses about 20 percent of your body's energy.

☐ **11.** Your eyes are incredible cameras. They can distinguish about 10 million different colors and process images faster than the best computers.

☐ **12.** Your taste buds are tiny but mighty. Your tongue has between 2,000 and 8,000 taste buds, each containing 50-100 taste cells.

☐ **13.** Your vocal cords are like musical instruments. They vibrate to produce sounds, and you can make thousands of different sounds with them.

☐ **14.** Your lungs are vital air factories. They have about 300 million tiny air sacs called alveoli, where oxygen enters your blood and carbon dioxide exits. You take about 20,000 breaths a day without even thinking about it.

☐ **15.** Your heart is a tireless worker. It beats about 115,000 times a day, pumping blood to all parts of your body. In a year, it pumps enough blood to fill a swimming pool.

☐ **16.** Your joints are like hinges. You have approximately 350 of them, allowing you to bend, twist, and move. But the smallest one is in your ear, where the stirrup bone helps transmit sound vibrations to your inner ear.

☐ **17.** During sleep, your brain cleanses itself of toxins, and your body repairs tissues and muscles. Plus, your eyes move rapidly during REM (rapid eye movement) sleep, which is when you dream.

☐ **18.** Water is crucial for your body's functions. About 60 percent of your body is water, and you lose about 8-12 cups of it every day through sweat, urine, and breathing.

☐ **19.** Inside your ear, there's a tiny balancing act. Your inner ear contains the vestibular system, helping you stay balanced. It's so sensitive that it can detect movements as small as 1/1,000th of a millimeter.

☐ **20.** On average, you blink about 15-20 times per minute. That's over 28,000 blinks per day. Blinking helps keep your eyes moist and clean, protecting them from dust and debris.

☐ **21.** Humans are covered in tiny hairs called vellus hair, but the longest strand of hair ever recorded was 18 feet 5.54 inches long, belonging to Xie Qiuping from China.

☐ **22.** Your saliva isn't just for wetting your mouth; it contains enzymes that kick-start digestion even before food reaches your stomach. On average, you produce about 2-7 cups of saliva each day.

☐ **23.** Your nose can detect over 1 trillion different scents. That's far more than the number of colors your eyes can see or the number of sounds your ears can hear. It's all thanks to the millions of olfactory receptors in your nasal cavity.

**24.** Goosebumps are your body's response to cold or emotional stimuli. When you're cold or scared, tiny muscles at the base of every hair follicle contract, which causes the hair to stand on end and create those familiar bumps.

**25.** Hiccups are caused by involuntary contractions of the diaphragm, the muscle beneath your lungs. While most hiccups go away on their own, some persistent cases can last for days, weeks, or even years.

# **Bonus**Fact

The hydrochloric acid in your stomach is so powerful that it can dissolve metal. Fortunately, the lining of your stomach is coated with a thick layer of mucus. This mucus prevents it from being digested by the acid.

# **Vocabulary**Builder

The masseter (*See No. 7*) is a powerful muscle in your jaw responsible for chewing food. It's one of the strongest muscles in your body relative to its size. When you bite down, the masseter contracts, moving your jaw up and down to grind and crush food before swallowing.

# Chapter 14
# Mind-blowing Mysteries

☐ **1.** The Bermuda Triangle, a region in the western area of the North Atlantic Ocean, is notorious for mysterious ship and plane disappearances. Despite numerous theories, including magnetic anomalies and methane gas eruptions, the true cause remains a puzzle.

☐ **2.** The Nazca Lines in Peru are massive geoglyphs etched into the desert floor. These 2,000-year-old designs depict various animals and shapes, visible only from the air. Their purpose remains a mystery, with theories ranging from religious rituals to astronomical calendars.

☐ **3.** The Voynich Manuscript, an ancient book filled with strange illustrations and an indecipherable script, has puzzled scholars for centuries. No one knows who wrote it, what language it's written in, or what its purpose is, adding to its enigmatic allure.

☐ **4.** Crop circles, intricate patterns appearing mysteriously overnight in fields of crops, have baffled scientists and enthusiasts alike. While some claim they're hoaxes, others believe they're of extraterrestrial origin or have mystical significance, sparking endless debate and speculation.

☐ **5.** Stonehenge, a prehistoric monument in England, consists of huge standing stones arranged in a circular formation. Despite extensive research, its purpose and the methods used to construct it remain shrouded in mystery, fueling theories ranging from ancient calendars to ceremonial sites.

☐ **6.** The Lost City of Atlantis, a legendary island civilization mentioned by the ancient Greek philosopher Plato, has captivated imaginations for centuries. While some believe it's a fictional tale, others speculate about its possible existence and the mysteries hidden beneath the ocean's depths.

☐ **7.** The mysterious "Wow! Signal," a strong radio signal detected in 1977 from space, remains unexplained. Its brief, intense burst of radio waves, seemingly from the direction of the Sagittarius constellation, sparked excitement among astronomers but has never been detected again.

☐ **8.** The Mary Celeste was an American ship found abandoned and adrift in the Atlantic Ocean in 1872. It remains one of maritime history's greatest mysteries. The crew vanished without a trace, leaving behind a perfectly intact vessel with all their belongings and supplies, prompting endless speculation about their fate.

☐ **9.** The Moai statues of Easter Island, towering stone figures that were carved by the Rapa Nui people, raise questions about their purpose and the methods used to transport them across the island. Some theories suggest they served as markers for sacred sites or represented ancestral spirits.

☐ **10.** The mystery of the "Taos Hum," a low-frequency humming sound heard by residents of Taos, New Mexico, since the early 1990s, continues to puzzle scientists. Despite efforts to identify its source, including geological surveys and psychological studies, the cause of this persistent sound remains elusive.

☐ **11.** The mysterious moving rocks of Death Valley's Racetrack Playa have puzzled scientists for decades. These large stones leave long trails behind them, seemingly moving on their own accord across the desert floor.

☐ **12.** The Great Sphinx of Giza, a colossal limestone statue with the head of a human and the body of a lion, raises questions about its age and original purpose. While most scholars believe it was built during the reign of Pharaoh Khafre around 2500 BCE, its exact origins and symbolic significance remain debated.

☐ **13.** The Oak Island Money Pit, a supposed buried treasure site off the coast of Nova Scotia, Canada, has been the subject of countless excavations and speculation for centuries. Despite numerous attempts to uncover its secrets, including elaborate booby traps and mysterious inscriptions, the treasure, if it exists, remains elusive.

☐ **14.** The mysterious Fairy Circles of Namibia, circular patches of bare earth surrounded by grass, have puzzled scientists for decades. While some theories attribute them to termite activity or competition for resources, no single explanation can fully account for their formation, adding to the intrigue of these natural phenomena.

☐ **15.** The Tunguska event of 1908, an explosion over Siberia, flattened over 770 square miles of forest. Despite extensive study, the cause, whether a meteorite or comet, remains uncertain, leaving behind a mysterious cosmic enigma.

☐ **16.** The Antikythera Mechanism, an ancient Greek device discovered in a shipwreck off the coast of Antikythera, is considered the world's first analog computer. Dating back over 2,000 years, its intricate gears and dials were used to track astronomical positions, yet its purpose and origin puzzle historians.

☐ **17.** The mysterious phenomenon of ball lightning, glowing spheres of electrical energy often observed during thunderstorms, continues to baffle scientists. Despite various theories attempting to explain its formation, the true nature and mechanisms behind ball lightning remain elusive.

☐ **18.** The disappearance of the Roanoke Colony in the late 16th century, where over 100 settlers vanished without a trace, remains a baffling historical mystery. The only clue found was the word "Croatoan," which was carved into a wooden post and sparked centuries of speculation about the fate of the lost colony.

☐ **19.** The mysterious phenomenon of Spontaneous Human Combustion (SHC), where individuals seemingly burst into flames without an external heat source, has puzzled scientists and investigators for centuries. Despite various theories, including natural explanations and paranormal phenomena, the true cause of SHC remains elusive.

☐ **20.** The phenomenon of the Marfa Lights, mysterious orbs of light appearing near Marfa, Texas, has puzzled observers for generations. Despite numerous scientific investigations, including theories of atmospheric conditions and geological factors, the true nature of these lights remains unexplained.

☐ **21.** The mystery of the Georgia Guidestones, a granite monument in Georgia, inscribed with 10 guidelines for humanity in eight different languages, has sparked curiosity and speculation since its erection in 1980. The creator's identity is unknown and  the purpose behind its messages remains a mystery. The monument was destroyed in 2022.

☐ **22.** The phenomenon of deja vu, the feeling of having experienced a situation before, continues to puzzle scientists and psychologists. Despite various theories, including memory glitches and neurological explanations, the true cause of deja vu remains uncertain, adding to its mysterious nature.

☐ **23.** The mysterious phenomenon of the "Taman Shud Case," also known as the Somerton Man mystery, involves an unidentified man found dead on Somerton Beach in Australia in 1948. With no identification and cryptic clues, including a torn scrap of paper with the words "Taman Shud," the case remains unsolved.

☐ **24.** The mystery of the Crystal Skulls, a collection of allegedly ancient crystal skulls found across the globe, has fueled speculation about their origin and purpose. Despite claims of mystical powers and connections to ancient civilizations, skeptics argue they are modern forgeries, adding to the enigma surrounding these artifacts.

☐ **25.** The phenomenon of St. Elmo's Fire, glowing plasma discharges appearing on the masts and rigging of ships during thunderstorms, has puzzled sailors for centuries. Despite scientific explanations involving electric fields and ionization, the eerie appearance of St. Elmo's Fire continues to captivate and mystify observers.

# **Bonus**Fact

The mystery of the Green Children of Woolpit, two children with green-tinted skin who appeared in the English village of Woolpit in the 12th century, remains a curious historical enigma. Despite various theories, including extraterrestrial origin or exposure to unknown substances, the true explanation behind their unusual appearance remains unknown.

# **Vocabulary**Builder

Geoglyphs (*See No. 2*) are large-scale designs or motifs created on the ground, typically using natural materials or shaping the landscape. Often found in desert regions, these ancient artworks can depict animals, shapes, or intricate patterns. They serve various purposes, from religious or ceremonial significance to marking territory or navigation aids.

# Chapter 15
# Spectacular Sports

☐ **1.** In basketball, the tallest NBA player ever was Gheorghe Mureşan, standing at a staggering 7 feet 7 inches tall.

☐ **2.** Baseball's shortest Major League Baseball game was only 51 minutes long. The New York Giants beat the Philadelphia Phillies 6-1 on Sept. 28, 1919.

☐ **3.** Football helmets weren't always mandatory. They were only required in the NFL beginning in 1943 due to an increase in head injuries.

☐ **4.** Hakan Suker of Turkey scored the fastest goal in soccer's World Cup. His goal came just 11 seconds after kickoff during a 2002 match featuring Turkey vs. South Korea.

☐ **5.** The longest recorded discus throw was by Jürgen Schult from Germany, hurling the discus a remarkable 243 feet in 1986.

☐ **6.** Ice hockey legend Wayne Gretzky held 61 NHL records, including most career goals and assists, when he retired in 1999.

☐ **7.** The highest score ever recorded in a single basketball game was 186-184. In 1983, the Detroit Pistons outscored the Denver Nuggets in triple overtime.

☐ **8.** In baseball, a pitcher can throw a knuckleball that may flutter unpredictably due to minimal spin, making it challenging for batters to hit.

☐ **9.** Football fields weren't always the standard size. In the early days, they could vary significantly until regulations standardized them in the late 19th century.

☐ **10.** Baseball's "Mendoza Line" refers to a batting average of .200, named after shortstop Mario Mendoza, who is known for his low batting average.

☐ **11.** In hockey, the "Original Six" refers to the six teams that formed the NHL before its expansion in 1967: Toronto Maple Leafs, Montreal Canadiens, Detroit Red Wings, Boston Bruins, Chicago Blackhawks, and New York Rangers.

☐ **12.** Soccer's World Cup trophy is made of 18-carat gold and weighs around 13 pounds. It's one of the most coveted prizes in sports. The World Cup trophy was once stolen. In 1966, it disappeared while on display in England but was later found by a dog named Pickles and his owner, David Corbett.

☐ **13.** In baseball, the fastest recorded pitch speed is a blistering 105.8 mph, thrown by Aroldis Chapman in 2010.

☐ **14.** Soccer's Cristiano Ronaldo is known for his incredible vertical leap, reportedly reaching heights of over 30 inches.

☐ **15.** The first Olympic Games were held in ancient Greece in 776 BC, featuring sports like running, wrestling, and chariot racing. The first modern Olympic Games were held in 1876 in Athens, Greece, reviving the ancient tradition of athletic competition.

☐ **16.** In track and field, the high jump world record is 8 ft 1/4 in, set by Javier Sotomayor of Cuba in 1993.

☐ **17.** The longest professional baseball game lasted 33 innings. The Pawtucket Red Sox defeated the Rochester Red Wings 3-2 in 1981.

☐ **18.** Soccer's "Hand of God" goal refers to Diego Maradona's controversial handball goal during the 1986 FIFA World Cup, which Maradona famously described as "a little with the head of Maradona and a little with the hand of God."

☐ **19.** In basketball, the NBA introduced the three-point line in the 1979-1980 season, forever changing the game's dynamics.

□ **20.** Baseball's Cy Young holds the record for the most career wins as a pitcher, with an astonishing 511 victories. Young was inducted into the National Baseball Hall of Fame in 1937.

□ **21.** Football's Vince Lombardi Trophy, awarded to the Super Bowl champion, is made by Tiffany & Co. and is valued at over $10,000.

□ **22.** Track and field's Usain Bolt holds the record for the fastest 100-meter dash, clocking in at an astonishing 9.58 seconds.

□ **23.** The term "hat trick" originated in cricket but is commonly used in hockey to describe someone who scores three goals in a single game.

□ **24.** Baseball's "Curse of the Bambino" refers to the alleged curse that plagued the Boston Red Sox after trading Babe Ruth to the New York Yankees in 1919.

□ **25.** Football's Vince Lombardi, after whom the Super Bowl trophy is named, coached the Green Bay Packers to five NFL championships in the 1960s.

# **Bonus**Facts

Football's "Fog Bowl" was a 1988 NFL playoff game featuring the Philadelphia Eagles and Chicago Bears, played in dense fog that obscured visibility.

Soccer's Pelé scored over 750 career goals and is widely regarded as one of the greatest footballers of all time.

Basketball's slam dunk was popularized by players like Julius Erving, whose high-flying acrobatics revolutionized the game.

# **Vocabulary**Builder

A knuckleball (*See No. 8*) is a pitch in baseball that moves unpredictably due to minimal spin. Unlike other pitches, it doesn't rotate much, causing it to flutter or wobble as it travels toward the batter. This erratic movement makes it difficult for batters to predict its trajectory, challenging them to make solid contact.

# Chapter 16
# Superheroes of STEM

## Science

☐ **1.** Known as the "Mother of Modern Physics," Marie Curie was the first woman to win a Nobel Prize. She is also the only person to win Nobel Prizes in two different sciences—Physics and Chemistry.

☐ **2.** Nikola Tesla, a brilliant inventor, claimed to receive ideas through vivid visions and dreams, contributing to groundbreaking discoveries in electricity and magnetism.

☐ **3.** Mae Jemison, the first African-American woman in space, is also a trained dancer and once appeared on the television show "Star Trek: The Next Generation."

☐ **4.** Albert Einstein, famous for his theory of relativity, had a love for sailing and once said, "I sail because it releases my mind from the tyranny of clocks and calendars."

☐ **5.** Jane Goodall, a renowned primatologist, discovered that chimpanzees use tools and have complex social behaviors, revolutionizing our understanding of animal intelligence.

☐ **6.** Rosalind Franklin's X-ray diffraction images of DNA played a critical role in the discovery of its double helix structure, although her contributions were initially overshadowed.

☐ **7.** Galileo Galilei, often called the "father of modern science," was an accomplished musician who played the lute and composed music.

## Technology

☐ **8.** Steve Wozniak, co-founder of Apple, built his first computer, the "Cream Soda Computer," at age 11, using spare parts from his father's workplace.

☐ **9.** Tim Berners-Lee, the inventor of the World Wide Web, originally proposed the idea to streamline communication between scientists.

☐ **10.** In addition to her Hollywood career, Hedy Lamarr co-invented a frequency-hopping technology used in modern wireless communication systems.

☐ **11.** Jack Kilby, inventor of the integrated circuit, carried a notebook with him at all times to jot down ideas, leading to his groundbreaking innovation.

☐ **12**. Ada Lovelace, often considered the first computer programmer, wrote the first algorithm for Charles Babbage's Analytical Engine.

☐ **13.** Elon Musk, founder of SpaceX and Tesla, taught himself computer programming at a young age and sold his first video game, Blastar, at 12.

# Engineering

☐ **14.** Emily Warren Roebling, instrumental in the completion of the Brooklyn Bridge, oversaw its construction after her husband, the chief engineer, fell ill. She became the first person to cross the completed Brooklyn Bridge, leading a procession of vehicles.

☐ **15.** George Washington Gale Ferris Jr. invented the Ferris wheel for the 1893 World's Columbian Exposition in Chicago.

☐ **16.** Mary Anderson patented the windshield wiper in 1903 after noticing drivers struggling to see through their carriages' windows during snowstorms.

☐ **17.** Katherine Johnson, an American mathematician and aerospace engineer, calculated trajectories for historic space missions at NASA, including the Apollo 11 moon landing.

☐ **18.** In 1926, American engineer Robert Goddard launched the world's first liquid-fueled rocket, laying the groundwork for modern rocketry.

☐ **19.** James Buchanan Eads, a self-taught engineer, designed and constructed the Eads Bridge over the Mississippi River, one of the earliest steel bridges in the U.S.

# Mathematics

☐ **20.** Euclid, known as the "Father of Geometry," wrote the "Elements," a comprehensive textbook on mathematics that remained a standard for over 2,000 years.

☐ **21.** Shakuntala Devi, known as the "Human Computer," displayed remarkable mental calculation abilities, including correctly multiplying two 13-digit numbers in seconds.

☐ **22.** Hypatia of Alexandria, an ancient mathematician, also taught philosophy and astronomy in Alexandria, Egypt.

☐ **23.** Fibonacci, an Italian mathematician from the Middle Ages, introduced the Hindu-Arabic numeral system to Europe and discovered the famous Fibonacci sequence.

☐ **24.** Carl Friedrich Gauss, known as the "Prince of Mathematicians," made significant contributions to number theory, algebra, statistics, and differential geometry.

☐ **25.** Pythagoras, an ancient Greek mathematician, formed the Pythagorean Brotherhood, a secret society dedicated to mathematical and philosophical study.

# **Bonus**Facts

Douglas Engelbart, inventor of the computer mouse, also developed early hypertext systems and video conferencing technologies.

Larry Page and Sergey Brin, co-founders of Google, initially named their search engine "BackRub" due to its ability to analyze backlinks.

# **Vocabulary**Builder

STEM refers to a group of academic disciplines: Science, Technology, Engineering, and Mathematics. It emphasizes interdisciplinary learning and problem-solving skills. Science explores the natural world, technology involves tools and processes, engineering designs and constructs, while mathematics provides the language and framework for understanding and quantifying patterns and relationships in these fields.

# Chapter 17
# Incredible Inventors

☐ **1.** Richard Gatling, inventor of the Gatling gun, was a pacifist who believed his invention would make wars so deadly that they would become obsolete.

☐ **2.** Bessie Nesmith Graham, mother of the Monkees' Michael Nesmith, invented Liquid Paper, a correction fluid, in 1951.

☐ **3.** Alfred Nobel, inventor of dynamite, established the Nobel Prize in his will to honor "those who, during the preceding year, have conferred the greatest benefit to humankind."

☐ **4.** Stephanie Kwolek, a chemist at DuPont, invented Kevlar, a super-strong material used in bulletproof vests and other protective gear.

☐ **5.** Theodor Seuss Geisel, known as Dr. Seuss, invented the word "nerd" in his book "If I Ran the Zoo."

☐ **6.** James Naismith, the inventor of basketball, initially used peach baskets for goals.

☐ **7.** Ruth Wakefield, inventor of the chocolate chip cookie, originally planned to make chocolate cookies but ran out of baker's chocolate, so she used broken-up Nestle chocolate bars instead.

☐ **8.** Temple Grandin, a renowned inventor and animal scientist, designed more humane livestock handling systems inspired by her autism and ability to think in pictures.

☐ **9.** Dr. Shirley Jackson, physicist and inventor, conducted breakthrough research in telecommunications, leading to the development of caller ID, call waiting, and fiber optic cables.

☐ **10.** George de Mestral, inspired by burrs sticking to his dog's fur during a walk, invented Velcro.

☐ **11.** Chester Greenwood, at age 15, invented earmuffs in 1877 to protect his ears while ice skating in Maine.

☐ **12.** Ruth Handler, co-founder of Mattel, invented the Barbie doll in 1959 after watching her daughter play with dolls made from paper.

☐ **13.** Percy Spencer, an engineer working on radar technology during World War II, accidentally discovered microwave cooking when a candy bar melted in his pocket.

☐ **14.** Lonnie Johnson, a NASA engineer, invented the Super Soaker water gun while working on a heat pump design.

☐ **15.** Josephine Cochran invented the dishwasher because she was tired of her fine china breaking during hand washing.

☐ **16.** Philo Farnsworth, who developed the first all-electric television system, envisioned electronic television at age 14 while plowing a field on his family's farm.

☐ **17.** Garrett Morgan, an African-American inventor, created the first traffic signal with a warning light in the early 20th century.

☐ **18.** John Pemberton, inventor of Coca-Cola, initially marketed it as a patent medicine, claiming it could cure ailments like headaches and impotence.

☐ **19.** Sarah E. Goode, one of the first African-American women to receive a patent, invented a folding cabinet bed, which was a precursor to the modern Murphy bed.

☐ **20.** Charles Macintosh, a Scottish chemist, invented waterproof fabric by sandwiching rubber between layers of cloth, which is known as the Mackintosh coat.

☐ **21.** Margaret E. Knight invented a safety device for textile looms at age 12 and later patented the paper bag machine.

☐ **22.** Dr. John Harvey Kellogg, creator of cornflakes, believed a bland diet, including cereal, could promote healthy living.

☐ **23.** Johannes Gutenberg, inventor of the printing press, faced financial ruin after a failed business venture but later revolutionized communication with his printing technology.

☐ **24.** Elizabeth Magie, creator of The Landlord's Game, a precursor to Monopoly, designed it to illustrate the pitfalls of capitalism and promote economic principles.

☐ **25.** John Walker, a pharmacist, accidentally invented the friction match in 1826 while stirring a mixture of chemicals on a stick.

# **Bonus**Facts

Margaret A. Wilcox, inventor of the car heater, was also a mechanical engineer and designed the first engine-powered vehicle heater.

Edwin Land, inventor of the Polaroid camera, came up with the idea while on vacation with his daughter, who asked why they couldn't see the photo immediately.

Granville Woods, known as the "Black Edison," held more than 50 patents, including one for the multiplex telegraph, which allowed trains to communicate with stations.

Brothers Orville and Wilbur Wright, known for inventing the airplane, made their own bicycles and repaired watches to fund their experiments.

Charles Goodyear, inventor of vulcanized rubber, spent years in debtors' prison due to his obsession with perfecting the process.

# **Vocabulary**Builder

Patent medicine (*See No. 18*) refers to unregulated remedies sold without prescription, often claiming to cure various ailments. Historically, these elixirs were widely advertised with exaggerated claims of effectiveness, sometimes containing undisclosed or harmful ingredients. They gained popularity in the 19th and early 20th centuries before regulations tightened to ensure safety and efficacy.

# Chapter 18
# Remarkable Robotics

☐ **1.** The Rubik's Cube-solving robot, "Sub1 Reloaded," can solve the iconic puzzle in just 0.637 seconds. Created by Albert Beer and his team, it uses specialized motors and algorithms to achieve lightning-fast solves.

☐ **2.** "Sophia," the humanoid robot developed by Hanson Robotics, was granted citizenship by Saudi Arabia in 2017, making her the first robot to receive citizenship in any country. Sophia can hold conversations, recognize faces, and even express emotions.

☐ **3.** Developed in 2016 by Boston Dynamics, "Spot" is a versatile quadruped robot designed for various tasks, including inspection, reconnaissance, and even dancing. Its advanced mobility and agility make it suitable for navigating challenging terrain and performing tasks in dynamic environments.

☐ **4.** "ASIMO," created by Honda, stands for Advanced Step in Innovative Mobility. This humanoid robot can walk, run, climb stairs, and even pour a drink. Its sleek design and sophisticated sensors enable it to interact with its surroundings and assist people in various ways.

☐ **5.** "Curiosity," NASA's Mars rover, has a robotic arm equipped with a drill and other scientific instruments to study the Martian surface. Since its landing on Aug. 6, 2012, Curiosity has been exploring the Red Planet, analyzing soil samples, and providing valuable data about Mars' geology and climate.

☐ **6.** The "Roomba," invented by Rodney Brooks and his team at iRobot, revolutionized household cleaning by autonomously vacuuming floors. Its intelligent navigation system maps the room to efficiently cover the area while avoiding obstacles.

☐ **7.** "Baxter," created by Rethink Robotics, is a robot designed to work alongside humans in manufacturing environments. With its friendly demeanor and adaptive capabilities, Baxter can perform various tasks, from assembly to packaging, enhancing productivity and safety in the workplace.

☐ **8.** "Robotic Fish," developed by MIT researchers, mimics the swimming motions of real fish to explore underwater environments and study marine life. Equipped with sensors and actuators, these bio-inspired robots can navigate tight spaces, monitor water quality, and collect data in areas inaccessible to traditional underwater vehicles.

☐ **9.** "Pepper," developed by SoftBank Robotics, is a humanoid robot designed to recognize emotions and engage in natural conversations with people. With its expressive features and AI-powered capabilities, Pepper serves as a companion and assistant in various settings, including retail stores and homes.

☐ **10.** The "International Space Station's Robotic Arm," also known as Canadarm2, plays a crucial role in assembling and maintaining the ISS. This robotic arm, built by the Canadian Space Agency, assists astronauts in capturing cargo spacecraft, conducting spacewalks, and moving equipment with precision.

☐ **11.** "RoboBees," developed by researchers at Harvard University, are tiny robotic insects inspired by the biology of bees. These micro-robots can fly and navigate autonomously, offering potential applications in pollination, environmental monitoring, and search-and-rescue missions.

☐ **12.** "Kismet," created by Dr. Cynthia Breazeal at MIT, is a social robot designed to interact with humans in emotionally intelligent ways. With its ability to recognize and respond to social cues, and its expressive face, Kismet paved the way for research in human-robot interaction and artificial empathy.

☐ **13.** Boston Dynamics' BigDog, developed in 2005, is a quadruped robot designed to traverse rough terrain with remarkable agility. Its dynamic stability and powerful locomotion enable it to carry heavy loads over uneven ground, making it suitable for military and civilian applications in challenging environments.

☐ **14.** "Robonaut," developed by NASA in collaboration with General Motors, is a humanoid robot designed to assist astronauts in space missions. Equipped with dexterous hands and advanced sensors, It can perform delicate tasks and operate tools in the International Space Station's microgravity environment.

☐ **15.** "PLEN2," a palm-sized humanoid robot developed by PLEN Project Company, is designed for educational and hobbyist purposes. With its open-source platform and modular design, PLEN2 allows users to explore robotics, programming, and 3D printing.

☐ **16.** The "Da Vinci Surgical System," developed by Intuitive Surgical, revolutionized minimally invasive surgery with its robotic-assisted technology. Surgeons control robotic arms equipped with surgical instruments and cameras, enabling precise movements and enhanced visualization during procedures. This leads to shorter recovery times and improved patient outcomes.

☐ **17.** "Mars Helicopter Ingenuity," a small autonomous rotorcraft deployed by NASA's Perseverance rover, achieved the first powered flight on another planet. This historic milestone demonstrated the feasibility of powered flight in the thin atmosphere of Mars, opening new possibilities for aerial exploration and reconnaissance in future missions.

☐ **18.** "DeepMind's AlphaGo," an AI program developed by Google's DeepMind, made headlines by defeating world champion Go players. AlphaGo's use of deep neural networks and reinforcement learning demonstrated significant advancements in AI's ability to tackle complex strategic games and solve real-world problems.

☐ **19.** "RHex," created by researchers at the University of Pennsylvania, is a rugged hexapod robot capable of traversing various terrains, including sand, snow, and rubble. With its agile locomotion and robust design, RHex has applications in search and rescue, exploration, and environmental monitoring in challenging environments.

☐ **20.** "Moley Robotics' Robotic Kitchen," equipped with robotic arms and hands, can cook thousands of recipes with precision and consistency. Controlled via a smartphone app or by selecting recipes from an online database, this innovative kitchen system automates meal preparation, offering convenience and culinary expertise at home.

☐ **21.** The "Tactile Telerobot," developed by Stanford University researchers, allows users to remotely control a robotic hand with tactile feedback. By integrating sensors and actuators, users can feel the texture and resistance of objects as the robot interacts with them, enabling more intuitive and immersive teleoperation experiences.

☐ **22.** "Nao," developed by SoftBank Robotics, is a humanoid robot designed for education and research. With its interactive capabilities and programmable behaviors, Nao can engage students in learning activities, teach programming concepts, and facilitate social interaction and communication skills development.

☐ **23.** "DexNet," developed by researchers at UC Berkeley, is a robotic grasping system capable of handling a wide variety of objects with dexterity and efficiency. Using deep learning algorithms, DexNet can analyze object geometry and determine optimal grasping strategies, advancing automation in manufacturing and logistics.

☐ **24.** "Atlas," developed by Boston Dynamics, is a humanoid robot known for its agility and athleticism. With its bipedal locomotion and dynamic balance, Atlas can navigate uneven terrain, perform acrobatic maneuvers, and even participate in obstacle courses, showcasing advancements in robot mobility and control.

☐ **25.** "Robotic Exoskeletons," such as the EksoGT from Ekso Bionics, assist individuals with mobility impairments in walking and rehabilitation. These wearable robotic devices provide powered assistance to the wearer's limbs, enabling enhanced mobility and independence for people with neurological conditions or spinal cord injuries.

# **Bonus**Fact

"ROS" (Robot Operating System), an open-source framework maintained by the Open Robotics organization, provides a flexible and robust platform for developing and controlling robots. With a vast library of tools and libraries, ROS enables researchers and developers to collaborate, experiment, and innovate in robotics across various domains and applications.

# **Vocabulary**Builder

A humanoid robot (*See No. 2*) is a machine designed to resemble and mimic human characteristics, such as appearance and movement. These robots typically have a head, torso, arms, and legs, allowing them to perform tasks in a manner similar to humans. Humanoid robots are often used in research, entertainment, and assistance roles.

# Chapter 19
# Extreme Explorers

☐ **1.** Ranulph Fiennes, the "World's Greatest Living Explorer," completed the first polar circumnavigation of Earth via both poles in 1982.

☐ **2.** The legendary mountaineer Reinhold Messner climbed all 14 of the world's 8,000-meter peaks without supplemental oxygen, completing his quest in 1986.

☐ **3.** Jacques Cousteau, the famed marine explorer, pioneered underwater exploration in the mid-20th century. His underwater adventures aboard the Calypso vessel unveiled the oceans' wonders, inspiring generations to appreciate and protect marine ecosystems.

☐ **4.** Colin O'Brady, an American explorer, was the first person to complete an unassisted, solo crossing of Antarctica in 2018. He completed the 921-mile coast-to-coast journey in 53 days.

☐ **5.** Sarah Marquis, a modern-day adventurer, trekked alone over 10,000 miles from Siberia to Australia, surviving encounters with wildlife and harsh environments.

☐ **6.** In 1999, Bertrand Piccard and Brian Jones completed the first nonstop balloon circumnavigation of the globe, traveling over 25,000 miles in 20 days.

☐ **7.** Sir David Attenborough, a renowned naturalist and broadcaster, has explored the world's ecosystems for over six decades, bringing the wonders of nature into homes worldwide through his documentaries.

☐ **8.** Ed Stafford walked the entire length of the Amazon River, covering more than 4,000 miles in 860 days, facing challenges from wildlife and hostile tribes.

☐ **9.** In 1953, Tenzing Norgay and Sir Edmund Hillary became the first climbers to reach the summit of Mount Everest.

☐ **10.** Laura Dekker, the youngest person to sail solo around the world, completed her journey at the age of 16 in 2012.

☐ **11.** Dian Fossey, an American zoologist, embarked on groundbreaking expeditions to study and protect mountain gorillas in Rwanda during the 1960s and 1970s. Her research shed light on the complex social structures of these endangered primates, leading to conservation efforts to safeguard their habitat.

☐ **12.** In 2001, Erik Weihenmayer, who is blind, summited Mount Everest, becoming the first blind person to reach the world's highest peak.

☐ **13.** Steve Fossett completed the first solo nonstop circumnavigation of the globe in a balloon in 2002.

☐ **14.** In 2005, Ellen MacArthur set the world record for the fastest solo circumnavigation of the globe, completing the journey in just over 71 days.

☐ **15.** David Hempleman-Adams, the British adventurer, completed the "Explorers Grand Slam" by reaching the North and South Poles and climbing the Seven Summits.

☐ **16.** Arved Fuchs and Reinhold Messner traversed Antarctica on foot in 1989-1990, covering over 2,800 kilometers in 92 days.

☐ **17.** Roz Savage rowed solo across the Atlantic, Pacific, and Indian Oceans, becoming the first woman to complete the "Big Three" ocean rows.

☐ **18.** Lewis Pugh completed the first swim across the North Pole in 2007, enduring freezing temperatures and shifting ice floes.

☐ **19.** Robert Swan and his son Barney Swan completed the first unassisted trek to the South Pole using only renewable energy in 2017-2018.

☐ **20.** Felicity Aston became the first woman to ski solo across Antarctica in 2012, covering over 1,000 miles in 59 days.

☐ **21.** Nellie Bly, a pioneering journalist, traveled around the world in 72 days in 1889-1890, setting a new record for circumnavigation.

☐ **22.** Fanny Bullock Workman, an early 20th-century explorer, set altitude records for women climbers in the Himalayas.

☐ **23.** In 1947, Thor Heyerdahl sailed across the Pacific Ocean on the Kon-Tiki, a balsa wood raft, testing his theory of pre-Columbian transoceanic contact.

☐ **24.** Yuichiro Miura, the oldest person to summit Mount Everest at the age of 80, achieved this feat in 2013, defying age barriers.

☐ **25.** Alain Robert, known as the "French Spider-Man," climbs skyscrapers without safety equipment, showcasing extraordinary feats of urban exploration.

# **Bonus**Facts

Hiram Bingham rediscovered the lost Inca city of Machu Picchu in 1911, sparking a renewed interest in Inca civilization.

Louis Rudd was the second person to complete a solo and unsupported journey across Antarctica. He completed his journey just two days after Colin O'Brady became the first person to complete the journey.

Gerlinde Kaltenbrunner is the first woman to climb all 14 of the world's 8,000-meter peaks without supplemental oxygen, achieving this feat in 2011.

Wangari Maathai, a Kenyan environmentalist, launched the Green Belt Movement in the late 1970s, empowering communities to plant trees and combat deforestation. Her grassroots activism earned her the Nobel Peace Prize in 2004, recognizing her efforts to promote environmental conservation and social justice.

# **Vocabulary**Builder

Circumnavigation (*See No. 1*) is the act of traveling all the way around a planet, usually by sea or air. It involves completing a journey that crosses all meridians of longitude, eventually returning to the starting point. Famous circumnavigations include Magellan's expedition, which proved the Earth's roundness, and modern solo voyages like those of Laura Dekker.

# Chapter 20
# Transportation Trivia

☐ **1.** Did you know one of the fastest supercars in the world, the Bugatti Chiron Super Sport 300+, can reach speeds of over 300 miles per hour? That's faster than many airplanes during takeoff.

☐ **2.** The first recorded instance of flight with a human pilot occurred in 1783 when the Montgolfier brothers launched a hot air balloon. Their balloon was first tested by carrying a sheep, duck, and rooster.

☐ **3.** In Japan, you can find the Shinkansen, also known as the bullet train, which can travel at speeds of nearly 200 miles per hour, making it one of the fastest trains in the world.

☐ **4.** The world's largest cruise ship, Icon of the Seas, was launched in 2024. With a gross tonnage of 248,663, it is 1,196.7 feet long and cost nearly $2 billion to construct.

☐ **5.** The largest operational airplane in the world, the Antonov An-225 Mriya, had a wingspan longer than a football field and could carry the equivalent of 10 battle tanks. It was destroyed during the Russian invasion of Ukraine.

☐ **6.** The Panama Canal, which allows ships to travel between the Pacific and Atlantic oceans without navigating around South America, saves vessels about 7,872 miles of travel compared to the previous routes.

☐ **7.** In Amsterdam, there are more bicycles than people. The city is famous for its extensive network of bike paths and bike-friendly infrastructure. There are an estimated 881,000 bikes in Amsterdam.

☐ **8.** The Concorde, a supersonic passenger airliner, flew at more than twice the speed of sound, allowing it to travel from New York to London in just three hours. The Concord was retired in 2003.

☐ **9.** One of the world's longest bridges, the Danyang–Kunshan Grand Bridge in China, stretches for over 100 miles and is part of the Beijing-Shanghai High-Speed Railway.

☐ **10.** The iconic London Underground, opened in 1863, is the world's oldest underground railway. It serves over 270 stations.

☐ **11.** The Trans-Siberian Railway is the longest railway line in the world, stretching nearly 6,000 miles from Moscow to Vladivostok, crossing eight time zones.

☐ **12.** The famous Venice canals are not just for gondolas; they serve as the city's primary mode of transportation, with water buses, water taxis, and even ambulances navigating the waterways.

☐ **13.** In 2018, Denise Muller-Korenek reached speeds of nearly 184 miles per hour on her bicycle at Utah's Bonneville Salt Flats. She achieved this speed by drafting behind a specially designed top-fuel dragster.

☐ **14.** The International Space Station (ISS) travels at a staggering speed of approximately 17,500 miles per hour, orbiting the Earth roughly every 90 minutes.

☐ **15.** The term "taxicab" originated from the words "taximeter" and "cabriolet," referring to the first horse-drawn carriages fitted with meters to measure fares.

☐ **16.** The invention of the wheel is estimated to have occurred around 3500 BCE. It revolutionized transportation and enabled the development of wheeled vehicles.

☐ **17.** The English Channel, separating England from France, is crossed by the Eurotunnel, a nearly 32-mile underwater tunnel that connects the two countries.

☐ **18.** The Boneyard is the world's largest airplane graveyard and is located in Tucson, Arizona. It is home to over 4,400 retired aircraft, including commercial jets, military planes, and helicopters.

☐ **19.** The longest continuous road in the world is the Pan-American Highway, spanning over 19,000 miles from Alaska to Argentina, with only a small gap in the Darién Gap between Panama and Colombia.

- ☐ **20.** The term "jaywalking" originated in the early 20th century when "jay" was slang for someone who was naive or foolish, referring to pedestrians who crossed streets carelessly.

- ☐ **21.** Singapore Airlines operates the longest non-stop commercial flight in the world. It travels from Singapore to New York City and covers a distance of over 9,500 miles in around 18 hours.

- ☐ **22.** The concept of electric cars is not new. In fact, the first electric car was built in the late 19th century by Thomas Parker, a British inventor who designed a rechargeable battery-powered vehicle.

- ☐ **23.** The fastest recorded speed on the water was achieved by the Spirit of Australia, a hydroplane boat, in 1978, when it reached 318 miles per hour on the Tumut River in Australia.

- ☐ **24.** Completed in 1869, the Transcontinental Railroad connected the East and West coasts of the United States, reducing travel time from months to just a week.

- ☐ **25.** The world's first commercial jet airliner, the de Havilland Comet, entered service in 1952, revolutionizing air travel with its faster speeds and higher altitudes compared to propeller-driven aircraft.

# **Bonus**Facts

The world's longest railway tunnel, the Gotthard Base Tunnel in Switzerland, stretches for over 35 miles through the Alps, providing a vital link for freight and passenger trains between northern and southern Europe.

The concept of a bicycle was first developed by Baron Karl von Drais in 1817. His invention, called the "running machine," had no pedals and was propelled by the rider pushing their feet against the ground.

# **Vocabulary**Builder

A hydroplane boat (*See No. 23*) is a specialized watercraft designed to skim across the water's surface. These boats achieve high speeds by reducing drag, allowing them to glide effortlessly over the water. Hydroplane racing is a popular sport showcasing these unique vessels' speed and agility.

# Chapter 21
# Ancient Achievements

☐ **1.** The Great Pyramid of Giza, built around 2560 BCE, was the tallest human-made structure for over 3,800 years. Its precision engineering allowed it to align accurately to the four main points (north, east, south, and west) on a compass.

☐ **2.** The Romans used a type of concrete that set underwater, enabling them to construct sturdy harbors and aqueducts. This ancient concrete is still stronger than its modern counterparts.

☐ **3.** The ancient Egyptians invented papyrus, a type of paper made from the papyrus plant. It revolutionized writing and record-keeping.

☐ **4.** The ancient city of Mohenjo-Daro in the Indus Valley in Pakistan had an advanced drainage system, complete with covered drains and soak pits.

☐ **5.** The Chinese built the Great Wall, which stretches over 13,000 miles, to protect against invasions from northern nomadic tribes.

☐ **6.** The Parthenon, a temple dedicated to the goddess Athena, was built in ancient Greece using innovative architectural techniques, including subtle curves and optical illusions to counteract visual distortions.

☐ **7.** The ancient Mayans developed sophisticated calendar systems, including the Long Count calendar, which accurately measured long periods of time.

☐ **8.** The Hanging Gardens of Babylon were an engineering marvel featuring lush vegetation cascading down terraces. They are one of the Seven Wonders of the Ancient World

☐ **9.** The city of Petra in Jordan was carved directly into rose-colored sandstone cliffs, showcasing incredible rock-cut architecture by the Nabataeans.

☐ **10.** The ancient Egyptians developed a system of writing called hieroglyphics, using pictures and symbols to represent words and sounds.

☐ **11.** The Mausoleum at Halicarnassus, built in the 4th century BCE, was an elaborate tomb for King Mausolus and featured intricate sculptures and reliefs. It is one of the Seven Wonders of the Ancient World.

☐ **12.** The Inca civilization constructed Machu Picchu, a breathtaking citadel nestled high in the Andes Mountains, using precise stonework without mortar.

☐ **13.** The city of Tenochtitlan, the capital of the Aztec Empire, was built on a series of artificial islands in Lake Texcoco, connected by causeways and canals.

☐ **14.** The Colosseum in Rome could be flooded to stage naumachiae, which are mock naval battles, for the entertainment of spectators.

☐ **15.** The ancient city of Teotihuacan in Mexico had a grid-like layout with wide avenues and impressive pyramids, indicating sophisticated urban planning.

☐ **16.** The Antikythera Mechanism is an ancient Greek analog computer that was used to predict eclipses and astronomical positions.

☐ **17.** The Acropolis in Athens housed several important ancient Greek buildings, including the iconic Parthenon and the Temple of Athena Nike.

☐ **18.** The Sumerians of Mesopotamia (c. 3500 BCE) developed one of the earliest forms of writing called cuneiform, which involved making wedge-shaped impressions on clay tablets.

☐ **19.** The Norse Vikings navigated the seas using sundials, stars, and landmarks, demonstrating remarkable maritime knowledge.

☐ **20.** The Lighthouse of Alexandria, built around 280 BCE, was one of the tallest structures of the ancient world and guided ships into the harbor with its beacon. It is one of the Seven Wonders of the Ancient World.

☐ **21.** The ancient Greeks invented the concept of a theater, where plays and performances were held to entertain and educate the public.

☐ **22.** The Sumerians built ziggurats, massive stepped pyramids, as religious temples and administrative centers in ancient Mesopotamia (current day Iraq and Syria).

☐ **23.** The ancient Indian mathematician Aryabhata calculated the value of Pi to four decimal places and proposed a heliocentric solar system model.

☐ **24.** The city of Pompeii was preserved in ash in 79 CE when Mount Vesuvius erupted, providing valuable insights into ancient Roman life and architecture.

☐ **25.** The Mesoamerican ballgame, played by ancient civilizations like the Maya and Aztec, involved hitting a rubber ball through stone rings without using hands or feet.

# **Bonus**Facts

The Nazca Lines in Peru are giant geoglyphs etched into the desert floor, depicting animals, plants, and geometric shapes. They were created by the Nazca civilization.

The ancient Babylonians developed a sophisticated system of mathematics, including the concept of zero and the base-60 numeral system still used for measuring time and angles.

The ancient Persians built an extensive network of royal roads spanning over 1,600 miles to facilitate communication and trade within their empire.

The Oracle of Delphi, located in ancient Greece, was consulted by people seeking advice and prophecy from the gods.

# **Vocabulary**Builder

Mesoamerican (*See No. 25*) refers to the diverse cultures that flourished in the region of present-day Mexico and parts of Central America before the arrival of Europeans. These civilizations, including the Maya, Aztec, and Olmec, shared common characteristics such as complex societies, advanced agriculture, and monumental architecture.

# Chapter 22
# Archaic Medicines

◻ **1.** Ancient Egyptians used honey as an antibacterial ointment for wounds, harnessing its natural healing properties. Honey's viscosity created a protective barrier, preventing infection and promoting tissue regeneration.

◻ **2.** In ancient Greece, physicians believed in the power of humorism, balancing bodily fluids or humors—blood, phlegm, yellow bile, and black bile—to maintain health. Imbalances were thought to cause illness.

◻ **3.** Mesoamerican civilizations like the Aztecs and Mayans used cocoa beans medicinally, brewing them into a bitter drink to treat ailments such as fever, coughs, and even diarrhea.

◻ **4.** Ancient Chinese medicine incorporated acupuncture, which involved inserting very thin needles into designated points on the body to regulate the flow of life energy and restore health and balance.

◻ **5.** In medieval Europe, the belief in the "Doctrine of Signatures" led to the use of plants resembling certain body parts to treat ailments in those areas. For example, walnuts, with their brain-like appearance, were used to treat headaches.

◻ **6.** Ancient Indian Ayurvedic medicine promoted the use of spices like turmeric and ginger for their anti-inflammatory and digestive properties, believing in the balance of bodily doshas for overall health.

◻ **7.** The ancient Romans used urine as a diagnostic tool, believing its taste, smell, and color could reveal insights into a person's health, such as diabetes or kidney problems.

◻ **8.** In ancient Persia, physicians like Avicenna developed intricate medical encyclopedias detailing various diseases, treatments, and surgical techniques, laying the foundation for modern medical knowledge.

☐ **9.** Ancient Babylonians practiced trepanation, a surgical procedure involving drilling holes into the skull to treat head injuries, relieve pressure, or even release evil spirits believed to cause mental illness.

☐ **10.** The ancient Greeks believed in the healing power of music, using melodies and rhythms to soothe patients' minds and bodies, promoting relaxation and aiding in the recovery process.

☐ **11.** Ancient Egyptian physicians used moldy bread to treat infected wounds, unknowingly harnessing the antibiotic properties of penicillin-producing mold spores to fight off harmful bacteria.

☐ **12.** In ancient Egypt, medical papyri dating back to around 1550 BCE contain detailed descriptions of surgical procedures, anatomical knowledge, and medicinal recipes used to treat various ailments.

☐ **13.** In ancient China, medicinal wines infused with herbs and spices were commonly used to treat a variety of ailments. They were believed to enhance the body's Qi and promote overall well-being.

☐ **14.** Ancient Greek physicians like Hippocrates emphasized the importance of exercise and diet in maintaining good health, prescribing specific foods and physical activities tailored to individual patients' needs.

☐ **15.** Mayan medicine practitioners used a combination of herbal remedies, sweat baths, and ritual ceremonies to treat illnesses, believing in the interconnectedness of the body, mind, and spirit.

☐ **16.** Ancient Egyptian physicians recognized the medicinal properties of garlic, using it to treat infections and digestive issues.

☐ **17.** In medieval Europe, barber-surgeons performed bloodletting—a practice believed to rebalance the body's humors—using leeches or lancets to draw blood from patients as a treatment for various ailments.

☐ **18.** Ancient Chinese medicine employed cupping therapy, which involved placing heated cups on the skin to create suction. This was believed to stimulate blood flow, relieve muscle tension, and promote healing.

☐ **19.** Ancient Roman physicians prescribed the consumption of crushed snails mixed with milk or wine as a remedy for coughs and respiratory ailments, attributing its effectiveness to the slimy texture soothing irritated throats.

☐ **20.** In ancient Greece, physicians used opium derived from the poppy plant as a pain reliever and sedative, often administered in the form of a drink or paste to alleviate discomfort during medical procedures.

☐ **21.** Ancient Indian Ayurvedic texts describe the use of ghee, or clarified butter, as a medicinal substance believed to promote digestion, strengthen the immune system, and nourish the body's tissues.

☐ **22.** In ancient Mesopotamia, clay tablets inscribed with medical prescriptions dating back to 2100 BCE detail remedies for various ailments, including gastrointestinal issues, skin conditions, and eye infections.

☐ **23.** Ancient Egyptian physicians utilized the medicinal properties of aloe vera to treat burns, wounds, and skin irritations, applying the gel-like substance directly to affected areas for its soothing and healing effects.

☐ **24.** In medieval Europe, the belief in sympathetic magic led to the use of medicinal amulets and talismans, which were believed to harness mystical powers to protect against illness and promote healing.

☐ **25.** Ancient Greek physicians like Galen stressed the importance of cleanliness and hygiene to prevent disease, and prompted practices such as bathing, handwashing, and environmental sanitation.

◆———————————————◆

# **Vocabulary**Builder

Papyri (*See No. 12*) are ancient documents made from papyrus, a material derived from the pith of the papyrus plant. These documents were commonly used in ancient Egypt and other Mediterranean civilizations to write letters, records, religious texts, and other written materials, providing valuable insights into ancient societies and cultures.

# Chapter 23
# Planet Earth

☐ **1.** The Earth's surface is made up of 71 percent water, but only 2.5 percent of that is freshwater, with the rest being saltwater oceans.

☐ **2.** Africa is the only continent situated in all four hemispheres—Northern, Southern, Eastern, and Western. It is also the second largest continent, covering approximately 11.7 million square miles—about one-fifth of the Earth's total land surface.

☐ **3.** The Pacific Ocean is the world's deepest and largest ocean. It is so vast that all continents could fit into it. It covers more than 60 million square miles.

☐ **4.** Mount Everest, the world's tallest peak at 29,031 feet, grows about 0.16 inches taller each year due to tectonic plate movement.

☐ **5.** Lake Baikal in Russia is the world's deepest lake, plunging to a depth of over 5,300 feet. It is estimated that Lake Baikal holds more than 20 percent of the unfrozen fresh water on the Earth's surface.

☐ **6.** Antarctica is the Earth's driest and coldest continent, with temperatures dropping as low as -128.6°F. It is the fifth largest continent, making up approximately 9.4 percent of the Earth's land mass.

☐ **7.** The highest waterfall on Earth is Angel Falls in Venezuela, plunging over 3,200 feet from the top of Auyán-tepui. For comparison, Niagara Falls is about 180 feet tall.

☐ **8.** The Great Barrier Reef is the Earth's largest living structure. It stretches more than 1,400 miles off the coast of Australia. It is composed of 900 islands and more than 2,900 individual reefs.

☐ **9.** The Nile River is the longest river in the world, flowing over 4,130 miles through northeastern Africa. The Amazon River is second at 4,000 miles.

□ **10.** Greenland has the world's largest ice sheet outside of Antarctica, covering about 80 percent of its landmass.

□ **11.** The Dead Sea, bordered by Jordan and Israel, is the lowest point on Earth's land surface, sitting at 1,358 below sea level. It is not a sea; it is actually a lake. It is so salty that it's nearly 10 times saltier than the ocean, making it impossible for most organisms to live in.

□ **12.** Earth's atmosphere is composed of approximately 78 percent nitrogen, 21 percent oxygen, and trace amounts of other gases.

□ **13.** The Sahara Desert in Africa is the largest hot desert in the world. It covers an area of more than 3.5 million square miles. Due to desertification caused by human activity and climate change, it is expanding by about half a mile each month.

□ **14.** The Mariana Trench in the Pacific Ocean is the deepest point on Earth, reaching over 36,000 feet. The Tonga Trench is second, at more than 35,000 feet deep.

□ **15.** The Earth's magnetic field, generated by the movement of the outer core's molten iron, protects the planet from harmful solar radiation. The Earth's magnetic field is constantly changing, with the magnetic North Pole slowly drifting over time.

□ **16.** Earth's rotation is gradually slowing down at a rate of about 1.8 milliseconds per century due to the gravitational forces of the Moon and other factors.

□ **17.** Lake Superior, one of North America's Great Lakes, is the world's largest freshwater lake by surface area and third largest by volume. Its surface area is nearly 32,000 square miles, about the size of South Carolina.

□ **18.** The Atacama Desert in South America is one of the driest places on Earth, with some areas receiving an average of less than 0.04 inches of rainfall per year.

□ **19.** The Grand Canyon in Arizona is over 270 miles long and up to 18 miles wide, carved by the Colorado River over millions of years. At its deepest point, it is nearly 6,000 feet deep—that's more than a mile.

☐ **20.** The concept of "Pangaea" suggests that all current continents were once connected in a supercontinent around 300 million years ago.

☐ **21.** The Galápagos Islands, famous for their unique wildlife and role in Charles Darwin's theory of evolution, are located over 560 miles off the coast of Ecuador.

☐ **22.** The largest earthquake ever recorded occurred in Chile in 1960, measuring a magnitude of 9.5 on the Richter scale. The largest earthquake ever recorded in the United States was the Great Alaska Earthquake of 1964, measuring a magnitude of 9.2 and lasting almost 5 minutes.

☐ **23.** The largest impact crater on Earth is the Vredefort Crater in South Africa, formed over 2 billion years ago and stretching over 110-190 miles in diameter.

☐ **24.** The highest temperature ever recorded on Earth was 134°F (56.7°C) in Furnace Creek Ranch, Death Valley, California, USA, in 1913.

☐ **25.** The driest place on Earth is the McMurdo Dry Valleys in Antarctica, where some areas haven't seen rain in millions of years.

# **Bonus**Facts

The "Ring of Fire" is a horseshoe-shaped zone around the Pacific Ocean known for its frequent earthquakes and volcanic activity.

The deepest underwater trench outside of the Pacific Ocean is the Puerto Rico Trench, reaching depths of over 27,000 feet in the Atlantic.

# **Vocabulary**Builder

Tectonic plates (*See No. 4*) are large, rigid pieces of Earth's outer shell that float on the semi-fluid asthenosphere beneath. They constantly move, causing earthquakes, volcanic eruptions, and the formation of mountains over millions of years. These movements result from the transfer of heat within the Earth and the force of mantle convection.

# Chapter 24
# Our Solar System

☐ **1.** The Sun makes up 99.8 percent of our solar system's mass, so big that over a million Earths could fit inside it.

☐ **2.** Jupiter's moon, Io, is the most volcanic body in our solar system, with more than 400 active volcanoes spewing sulfur and lava. Io is Jupiter's third-largest moon.

☐ **3.** Saturn's rings aren't solid; they consist of billions of pieces of ice and rock, varying in size from a grain of sand to a small car.

☐ **4.** Neptune's moon, Triton, is the only large moon in our solar system with a retrograde orbit—meaning it orbits in the opposite direction of Neptune's rotation.

☐ **5.** The Great Red Spot is a massive storm on Jupiter's surface. It is believed to have been raging for at least 400 years, possibly much longer.

☐ **6.** Venus rotates in the opposite direction to most other planets, so if you were standing on its surface, the Sun would rise in the west and set in the east.

☐ **7.** Uranus is tilted on its side, so its north and south poles are where other planets have their equators. Scientists believe a collision with a massive object might have caused this tilt.

☐ **8.** Mercury is the closest planet to the Sun and has the greatest temperature changes, swinging from -290°F at night to 800°F during the day.

☐ **9.** Mars has the tallest volcano in the solar system, Olympus Mons, which is about 13.6 miles high—nearly three times the height of Mount Everest.

☐ **10.** The asteroid belt between Mars and Jupiter is less crowded than you might think; there's a lot of space between asteroids, so spacecraft can safely navigate through it.

☐ **11.** Pluto was once believed to be our solar system's ninth planet. However, in 2006, it was reclassified as a dwarf planet because it didn't meet all the criteria required to be considered a full-fledged planet.

☐ **12.** Ganymede, one of Jupiter's moons, is the largest moon in our solar system—larger than the planet Mercury. It has its own magnetic field, making it the only moon in the solar system known to have one.

☐ **13.** Saturn's moon, Titan, has a thick atmosphere made mostly of nitrogen, with lakes and rivers of liquid methane and ethane on its surface. Titan is just one of Saturn's 82 moons.

☐ **14.** The Kuiper Belt is a region of the solar system beyond Neptune's orbit that's filled with icy objects, including Pluto and other dwarf planets.

☐ **15.** The Oort Cloud is a vast sphere of icy bodies surrounding the solar system, extending nearly halfway to the nearest star. It's thought to be the source of long-period comets.

☐ **16.** The asteroid Vesta is so massive that it's responsible for about 9 percent of the total mass of the entire asteroid belt.

☐ **17.** The surface of Venus is incredibly hot, reaching up to 900°F, enough to melt lead. It is the hottest planet in the solar system, even hotter than Mercury, which is the planet closest to the Sun.

☐ **18.** One of the largest known impact craters in the solar system is the South Pole-Aitken Basin on the moon, which is about 1,550 miles wide.

☐ **19.** The Sun's outer atmosphere, called the corona, is hundreds of times hotter than its surface, reaching temperatures of over 2,000,000°F. The surface temperature is about 10,000°F.

☐ **20.** Mercury's surface is covered in craters, much like the moon's, because it lacks an atmosphere to protect it from impacts.

☐ **21.** Phobos, one of Mars's moons, is slowly getting closer to the planet and is predicted to eventually break apart due to gravitational forces.

☐ **22.** Neptune's moon, Triton, is one of the coldest known objects in the solar system, with surface temperatures dropping as low as -391°F.

☐ **23.** Jupiter's moon, Callisto, is the most heavily cratered object in the solar system, indicating its ancient surface has remained relatively unchanged for billions of years.

☐ **24.** The rings of Uranus are dark and narrow, making them difficult to see from Earth, especially compared to the bright, wide rings of Saturn.

☐ **25.** The dwarf planet Ceres is the largest object in the asteroid belt. It was recently visited by the NASA Dawn spacecraft.

# **Bonus**Facts

Saturn's moon, Mimas, has a large crater called Herschel that resembles the Death Star from Star Wars, earning it the nickname "the Death Star moon."

Europa, one of Jupiter's 95 moons, has an ocean beneath its icy crust, making it a promising place to search for extraterrestrial life.

Mars' Valles Marineris is a vast canyon system stretching over 2,500 miles long and up to 7 miles deep, dwarfing the Grand Canyon on Earth.

The Moon's lack of atmosphere means there's no weather to erode the footprints left by astronauts, preserving them for millions of years.

The rings of Saturn were first observed by Galileo in 1610, but their true nature as separate ring structures wasn't understood until later observations.

# **Vocabulary**Builder

A dwarf planet (*See No. 11*) is a type of celestial object that orbits the Sun and is spherical in shape due to its own gravity, but it has not cleared its orbital path of other debris, like a true planet. It is smaller than a planet and may share its orbit with other similar-sized objects.

# Chapter 25
# The Milky Way

☐ **1.** The Milky Way is estimated to be about 13.6 billion years old, nearly as old as the universe itself, making it one of the oldest galaxies.

☐ **2.** The Milky Way galaxy is shaped like a giant, rotating disk with a bulging center. Spiral arms extend from the center, where stars and gas are concentrated. Surrounding the disk is a halo of stars and dark matter.

☐ **3.** The Milky Way travels through space at an astonishing speed of about 1.3 million miles per hour, dragging our solar system along for the ride.

☐ **4.** In ancient times, the Milky Way was often called the "Silver River" or "River of Heaven" by various cultures, inspired by its milky appearance stretching across the night sky.

☐ **5.** The Milky Way is home to an estimated 100 billion to 400 billion stars, each with its own unique characteristics and history.

☐ **6.** The Milky Way is so vast that light takes about 100,000 years to travel from one end of the galaxy to the other.

☐ **7.** The Milky Way's disk contains a population of variable stars known as Cepheid variables. These stars pulsate in brightness over regular intervals and are used by astronomers to measure cosmic distances.

☐ **8.** The Milky Way is a barred spiral galaxy characterized by a central bar-shaped structure with spiral arms extending outward.

☐ **9.** The center of the Milky Way hosts a supermassive black hole called Sagittarius A*, which is about 4.3 million times the mass of our Sun.

☐ **10.** If our solar system were the size of a quarter, the Milky Way galaxy would be the size of the United States.

☐ **11.** The closest star to Earth in the Milky Way is Proxima Centauri, located in the Alpha Centauri star system, approximately 4.24 light-years away. Proxima Centauri is a red dwarf star that is much cooler and smaller than our Sun.

☐ **12.** The Milky Way's spiral arms are not static; they constantly move and evolve, with stars being born, living, and dying within them over millions of years.

☐ **13.** The Milky Way's name comes from its appearance as a milky band of light stretching across the night sky caused by the combined light of countless stars.

☐ **14.** Our solar system orbits the center of the Milky Way at a distance of about 27,000 light-years, taking roughly 225-250 million years to complete one orbit.

☐ **15.** The Milky Way contains vast interstellar gas and dust regions, which can block visible light but emit radio waves, allowing astronomers to study these obscured regions.

☐ **16.** The Milky Way's central bulge contains a dense concentration of stars, including older populations and a high density of red giants.

☐ **17.** The Milky Way is part of a larger cosmic structure called the Local Group, which also includes the Andromeda Galaxy, the Triangulum Galaxy, and several smaller galaxies.

☐ **18.** The Milky Way is on a collision course with the Andromeda Galaxy. It is expected to merge with it in about 4 billion years, forming a new, larger galaxy nicknamed "Milkomeda."

☐ **19.** Our solar system is located in the Orion Arm of the Milky Way, about two-thirds of the way from the center to the edge.

☐ **20.** The Milky Way's disk contains spiral arms where most of the galaxy's star formation occurs, fueled by the compression of gas and dust as the arms sweep through.

☐ **21.** The Milky Way's central bulge is thought to be shaped like a peanut due to the combined gravitational forces of stars orbiting in elongated paths.

☐ **22.** The Milky Way's disk is not perfectly flat; it has a slight warp, with the outer regions bending upwards, likely due to interactions with satellite galaxies and dark matter.

☐ **23.** The study of the Milky Way's history and structure began in ancient times, with early astronomers like Hipparchus and Galileo observing its appearance and making rudimentary measurements.

☐ **24.** In the 18th and 19th centuries, astronomers such as William Herschel and William Parsons (Lord Rosse) used telescopes to map the Milky Way's shape and identify nebulae and star clusters within it.

☐ **25.** In the 20th century, astronomers like Harlow Shapley and Edwin Hubble made groundbreaking discoveries about the Milky Way's structure, including its position within the universe and the existence of other galaxies beyond it.

# **Bonus**Facts

Modern astronomers use advanced instruments and telescopes, such as the Atacama Large Millimeter/submillimeter Array (ALMA) and the Hubble Space Telescope, to study the Milky Way's history, structure, and dynamics in unprecedented detail.

The Milky Way contains a population of stars known as hypervelocity stars. These stars travel at speeds exceeding the galaxy's escape velocity. They are likely ejected from the galactic center by the gravitational pull of the central supermassive black hole.

The Milky Way contains a population of pulsars, neutron stars that rapidly rotate and emit beams of radiation that move across the sky like lighthouse beams, which are detected as regular pulses of radio waves.

# **Vocabulary**Builder

A light-year (*See No. 14*) is a unit of distance used in astronomy, representing the distance that light travels in one year. Since light travels at a constant speed of about 186,282 miles per second in a vacuum, one light-year is approximately 5.879 trillion miles.

# Chapter 26
# The Universe

☐ **1.** The Universe is about 13.8 billion years old. Scientists estimate its age by studying the oldest light in the cosmos, called cosmic microwave background radiation. By analyzing this ancient light, scientists can determine the Universe's age and unravel its cosmic timeline.

☐ **2.** There are estimated to be approximately 100 billion galaxies in the observable Universe. It is believed that each galaxy contains billions to trillions of stars. The Universe is like a vast cosmic tapestry woven from countless celestial threads.

☐ **3.** The Great Wall is not just a structure on Earth; it's also the name of a vast cosmic structure—the Hercules-Corona Borealis Great Wall—stretching over 10 billion light-years across the Universe.

☐ **4.** The "Impossible" Black Hole in M87 is four times larger than our entire solar system. Its event horizon is so large that it could engulf the entire orbit of Neptune.

☐ **5.** The Boötes Void is an immense, nearly empty region of space spanning 330 million light-years across, with significantly fewer galaxies than other parts of the Universe.

☐ **6.** Some stars pulsate in size due to internal processes. These "pulsating variable stars" expand and contract, changing their brightness rhythmically over time.

☐ **7.** Gliese 436 b is a planet made of burning ice. Its high pressure and temperature cause its ice to remain solid while burning with blue flames.

☐ **8.** The cosmic web is a vast network of filaments made of dark matter and gas that spans the entire Universe and shapes the distribution of galaxies.

☐ **9.** Magnetars are neutron stars with incredibly strong magnetic fields. Magnetars have a magnetic field estimated to be one thousand trillion times the strength of Earth's magnetic field.

☐ **10.** There's a planet-sized diamond in the Centaurus constellation named "BPM 37093" or "Lucy." It's a crystallized white dwarf star with a diamond core.

☐ **11.** The Voyager 1 spacecraft, launched in 1977, is the first human-made object to reach interstellar space. It crossed the boundary of our solar system in 2012. As of January 2024, it was about 15 billion miles (136 Astronomical Units) from the Sun.

☐ **12.** The "Great Attractor" is a mysterious gravitational anomaly pulling our galaxy and millions of others toward it. Its exact nature remains unknown.

☐ **13.** Cosmic voids are vast regions of space almost entirely devoid of matter. They can be millions of light-years across and are critical for understanding the Universe's large-scale structure.

☐ **14.** The coldest known place in the Universe is the Boomerang Nebula, where temperatures drop to a bone-chilling -457°F.

☐ **15.** White holes are theoretical regions of space-time where nothing can enter from the outside, but matter and light can escape. They're the opposite of black holes.

☐ **16.** The "Hubble Ultra-Deep Field" image captured by the Hubble Space Telescope reveals thousands of galaxies in a tiny patch of sky, each containing billions of stars.

☐ **17.** The "Fermi Bubbles" are two enormous gamma-ray-emitting bubbles extending 25,000 light-years below and above the Milky Way's galactic plane. They were possibly caused by a burst of star formation or activity around the supermassive black hole.

☐ **18.** Dark energy, comprising about 70 percent of the Universe's energy density, is driving its accelerated expansion. Its nature remains one of the biggest mysteries in cosmology.

☐ **19.** Rogue planets wander the Universe without orbiting a star. They drift through space untethered, potentially harboring life in the darkness between the stars.

☐ **20.** Hypervelocity stars travel at speeds exceeding 1 million miles per hour. They are ejected from the Milky Way's center by the gravitational pull of a supermassive black hole.

☐ **21.** Gamma-ray bursts are the most energetic events in the Universe. They release as much energy in a few seconds as the Sun will emit over its entire 10-billion-year lifetime.

☐ **22.** Quasars are incredibly distant and bright celestial objects powered by supermassive black holes at their centers. They often outshine entire galaxies.

☐ **23.** The "Wow! signal" was a strong, unexplained radio signal detected in 1977, lasting 72 seconds, originating from the direction of the Sagittarius constellation. Its source remains unidentified.

☐ **24.** Some galaxies, known as "cannibal galaxies," consume smaller galaxies through a process called galactic cannibalism, merging them into larger structures.

☐ **25.** The Universe might be a "Multiverse," containing many parallel universes with different physical laws and constants, offering potential explanations for the fine-tuning of our Universe.

# **Bonus**Facts

In a phenomenon called "gravitational lensing," massive objects like galaxies bend and distort light, acting as cosmic magnifying glasses and allowing us to observe distant objects otherwise too faint to see.

Some stars are composed almost entirely of metal, unlike the predominantly hydrogen and helium composition of most stars. These "metal stars" challenge traditional stellar evolution theories.

# **Vocabulary**Builder

An astronomical unit (AU) (*See No. 11*) is a measurement used in astronomy to describe distances. One AU is the average distance between the Sun and the Earth, which is about 93 million miles. It's a handy unit for understanding the distance of celestial objects.

# Chapter 27
# NASA News

☐ **1.** NASA was established on July 29, 1958, as a response to the launch of Sputnik 1, the Soviet Union's first artificial satellite, marking the beginning of the space race.

☐ **2.** Katherine Johnson, an African-American mathematician, calculated trajectories for the first American in space, the first American to orbit Earth, and the Apollo 11 moon landing.

☐ **3.** The Mercury program, NASA's first human spaceflight program, aimed to put Americans in space. It began in 1958 and lasted until 1963, with six crewed missions.

☐ **4.** NASA's Space Shuttle program, operational from 1981 to 2011, featured reusable spacecraft that carried astronauts and payloads to space, launching a new era of space exploration.

☐ **5.** Voyager 1 and Voyager 2, launched in 1977, are the farthest human-made objects from Earth. They continue to explore interstellar space, carrying messages about humanity on golden records.

☐ **6.** The Hubble Space Telescope, launched in 1990, has provided breathtaking images and transformed our understanding of the universe, revolutionizing astrophysics and cosmology.

☐ **7.** The Curiosity rover, part of the Mars Science Laboratory mission, landed on Mars in 2012 to assess its habitability and search for signs of past life. It made significant discoveries about the Red Planet.

☐ **8.** NASA's Artemis program aims to return humans to the moon, landing the first woman and the next man on the lunar surface by the mid-2020s, paving the way for future Mars missions.

☐ **9.** The International Space Station (ISS), a collaborative effort involving NASA, Russia, Europe, Japan, and Canada, serves as a laboratory for scientific research in space.

☐ **10.** The Mars Perseverance rover, launched in 2020, is looking for signs of past microbial life on Mars, collecting samples for potential return to Earth, and testing technology for future human missions.

☐ **11.** Gene Kranz, the flight director for Apollo 13, famously said, "Failure is not an option," as NASA worked tirelessly to safely bring the astronauts back to Earth after an explosion on the Apollo Service Module.

☐ **12.** NASA's Space Launch System (SLS) is its next-generation heavy-lift rocket. It is designed to carry astronauts to the moon and eventually to Mars, providing the capability for deep space exploration.

☐ **13.** NASA's Chandra X-ray Observatory, launched in 1999, observes X-rays from high-energy regions of the universe, revealing black holes, supernova remnants, and other exotic cosmic phenomena.

☐ **14.** The Juno spacecraft, launched in 2011, is studying Jupiter's composition, gravity field, magnetic field, and polar magnetosphere, shedding light on the planet's formation and evolution.

☐ **15.** The Pioneer 10 and 11 spacecraft, launched in 1972 and 1973, are the first human-made spacecraft to traverse the asteroid belt and make direct observations of Saturn and Jupiter

☐ **16.** NASA's Earth Observing System (EOS) satellites monitor Earth's climate, atmosphere, land, and oceans, providing valuable data for understanding and addressing environmental challenges.

☐ **17.** The New Horizons spacecraft, launched in 2006, performed a historic flyby of Pluto in 2015, providing the first detailed images and data of the distant dwarf planet and its moons.

☐ **18.** The Apollo Lunar Module, or "LEM," was the spacecraft used to land astronauts on the moon's surface during the Apollo missions. It consisted of a descent stage and an ascent stage.

☐ **19.** NASA's Kepler Space Telescope, launched in 2009, discovered thousands of exoplanets orbiting other stars, revolutionizing our understanding of planetary systems and the prevalence of Earth-like worlds.

☐ **20.** The Mars InSight lander, launched in 2018, is studying the interior of Mars, including its seismology and heat flow, to better understand the planet's geological history and evolution.

☐ **21.** NASA's Commercial Crew Program partners with private companies like SpaceX to transport astronauts to and from the ISS, reducing reliance on Russian Soyuz spacecraft.

☐ **22.** The X-15 rocket plane, flown by NASA and the U.S. Air Force from 1959 to 1968, set speed and altitude records.

☐ **23.** The Deep Space Network (DSN) is a global network of antennas that supports interplanetary spacecraft missions, providing communication and tracking services for missions throughout the solar system.

☐ **24.** The Apollo Lunar Roving Vehicle (LRV), or "moon buggy," allowed astronauts on Apollo 15, 16, and 17 to explore the lunar surface more extensively and cover greater distances.

☐ **25.** The "Astronomy Picture of the Day" (https://apod.nasa.gov/apod/) is a NASA website showcasing a different astronomical image or photograph each day, along with a brief explanation written by professional astronomers.

# **Bonus**Fact

The International Space Station (ISS) travels at a speed of nearly 17,500 miles per hour and orbits Earth approximately every 90 minutes. This allows astronauts to experience 16 sunrises and sunsets each day.

# **Vocabulary**Builder

NASA, the National Aeronautics and Space Administration, is the U.S. agency responsible for the nation's civilian space program and for aeronautics and aerospace research. Established in 1958, NASA conducts space exploration, scientific research, and technological innovation to advance understanding of the universe and benefit humanity.

# Chapter 28
# American Astronauts

☐ **1.** Sally Ride was America's first woman in space. In 1983, she flew aboard the Space Shuttle Challenger, inspiring girls worldwide to pursue careers in STEM fields.

☐ **2.** During the early days of space travel, astronauts consumed food in toothpaste-like tubes to prevent crumbs from floating in microgravity.

☐ **3.** The Apollo 11 mission, with Neil Armstrong, Buzz Aldrin, and Michael Collins, achieved the first manned moon landing on July 20, 1969.

☐ **4.** In 1962, John Glenn became the first American to orbit Earth aboard Friendship 7, circling the planet three times in just under five hours.

☐ **5.** After returning from the moon, Apollo 11 astronauts spent 21 days in quarantine to ensure they didn't bring back any space germs.

☐ **6.** Alan Shepard became the first American in space aboard Freedom 7 in 1961, a suborbital flight lasting 15 minutes and reaching a peak altitude of 116 miles.

☐ **7.** Peggy Whitson holds the record for the longest cumulative time spent in space by an American astronaut, with a total of 665 days over three missions aboard the ISS.

☐ **8.** Ed White became the first American to perform a spacewalk, or extravehicular activity (EVA), during the Gemini 4 mission in 1965, spending 23 minutes outside the spacecraft.

☐ **9.** Astronauts aboard the Space Shuttle used a special "restraint system," resembling a sleeping bag attached to the wall, to sleep in zero gravity.

☐ **10.** The oldest astronaut to fly in space was John Glenn, who returned to space aboard the Space Shuttle Discovery when he was 77.

☐ **11.** Jim Lovell, commander of Apollo 13, famously uttered the phrase "Houston, we have a problem" when their spacecraft encountered a critical failure.

☐ **12.** Alan Shepard, the first American in space, famously smuggled a makeshift golf club onto Apollo 14 and hit a golf ball on the lunar surface.

☐ **13.** In 1995, Eileen Collins became the first female Space Shuttle pilot. In 1999 she became the first female Space Shuttle commander leading the STS-93 mission aboard Columbia.

☐ **14.** Mae Jemison became the first African-American woman in space in 1992 when she flew aboard the Space Shuttle Endeavour as a mission specialist on STS-47, conducting scientific experiments.

☐ **15.** Astronauts on the Mercury missions were nicknamed "spam in a can" because of the cramped quarters and limited mobility inside their spacecraft.

☐ **16.** On Apollo 16, astronaut Charles Duke left a family portrait on the moon with a message: "This is the family of astronaut Duke from Planet Earth. Landed on the moon, April 1972."

☐ **17.** Astronauts on the Apollo missions collected over 800 pounds of moon rocks, which are still being studied by scientists today.

☐ **18.** Gemini 7 astronauts Wally Schirra and Thomas Stafford famously brought along a harmonica and bells and played "Jingle Bells" during a live broadcast from space on Dec. 16, 1965.

☐ **19.** Astronauts aboard the Space Shuttle Challenger conducted the first satellite repair mission in 1984, successfully fixing the malfunctioning Solar Maximum Mission satellite.

☐ **20.** In 1995, astronauts aboard the Space Shuttle Atlantis conducted the first docking with the Russian space station Mir, marking a milestone in international space cooperation.

☐ **21.** Astronauts aboard the Skylab space station conducted experiments on the effects of weightlessness on spiders, observing changes in their web-building behavior.

☐ **22.** Astronauts on long-duration missions experience changes in their vision due to fluid shifts in microgravity.

☐ **23.** In 1968, on Apollo 8, astronauts Frank Borman, Jim Lovell, and Bill Anders became the first humans to travel to and orbit the moon.

☐ **24.** Astronauts aboard the Space Shuttle used a special "space pen" developed by NASA to write in zero gravity.

☐ **25.** During the Gemini missions, astronauts drank specially formulated orange-flavored beverages to combat dehydration in space.

# **Bonus**Facts

John Young smuggled a corned beef sandwich into space during the Gemini 3 mission, surprising his fellow astronaut Gus Grissom.

On Apollo 12, astronauts Pete Conrad and Alan Bean inadvertently destroyed their TV camera by pointing it at the sun.

Gene Cernan, the last man to walk on the moon, left his daughter's initials, "TDC," written in the lunar dust.

From Its launch on May 14, 1973, until the return of its third and final crew on Feb. 8, 1974, the Skylab program proved that humans can live and work in outer space for extended periods of time. The final Skylab crew spent 84 days in space. On July 11, 1979, Skylab re-entered the Earth's atmosphere and disintegrated,

# **Vocabulary**Builder

Suborbital flight (*See No. 6*) is when a spacecraft briefly enters space but doesn't complete a full orbit around a celestial body, such as Earth. Instead, it follows a ballistic trajectory, reaching the edge of space before returning to the planet's surface. Suborbital flights are typically shorter and don't achieve the velocity needed for orbit.

# Chapter 29
# Creative Cuisines

☐ **1.** In Japan, you can find a delicacy called "fugu," a pufferfish dish that can be deadly if not prepared correctly. Specially trained chefs meticulously remove the poisonous parts, leaving behind safe, delicious meat.

☐ **2.** In Mexico, "chapulines" are toasted grasshoppers seasoned with salt, lime, and chili. They're a popular snack enjoyed for their crunchy texture and nutty flavor, often eaten on their own or sprinkled over dishes like tacos.

☐ **3.** Ever heard of "hákarl"? It's an Icelandic dish consisting of fermented shark meat. Due to its strong ammonia smell and taste, hákarl is an acquired taste even for the bravest food adventurers.

☐ **4.** Bhutanese cuisine boasts "ema datshi," a spicy dish made with chili peppers and yak cheese. Locals love its fiery kick, but it might be too hot to handle for some.

☐ **5.** South Korea offers "beondegi," a snack made from steamed silkworm pupae. Rich in protein and nutrients, it's a crunchy treat enjoyed by many, though its appearance might make you think twice.

☐ **6.** Have you ever tried "durian," known as the king of fruits? Native to Southeast Asia, this spiky fruit is famous for its pungent odor, often described as a mix of rotten onions and turpentine. Despite its smell, its custardy flesh is adored by many.

☐ **7.** China's "century egg" isn't actually a century old, but it's aged for weeks or months in a mixture of salt, ash, clay, quicklime, and rice hulls. The result? A translucent egg with a creamy, pungent flavor.

☐ **8.** Love cheese? Then you might be intrigued by "casu marzu," a Sardinian delicacy featuring sheep's milk cheese infested with live maggots.

☐ **9.** In parts of Africa, "fufu" is a popular staple made from boiled and pounded starchy ingredients like cassava, yams, or plantains. It's often served with savory soups or stews and eaten by hand, rolled into small balls.

☐ **10.** "Akutaq" is a traditional Inuit dessert made from whipped animal fat mixed with berries, fish, or other local ingredients.

☐ **11.** "Escamoles" are ant larvae harvested from the roots of agave plants in Mexico. Often dubbed "insect caviar," these creamy morsels are prized for their nutty flavor.

☐ **12.** Native to Australia, "witchetty grubs" are large, white moth larvae traditionally eaten by Indigenous Australians. Rich in protein and fat, they can be eaten raw or lightly cooked and are said to taste like almonds.

☐ **13.** Norway's "lutefisk" is made from dried whitefish soaked in a lye solution, then rehydrated and cooked. Despite its pungent smell, its gelatinous texture and mild flavor make it a holiday favorite for many Norwegians.

☐ **14.** In Peru, you can find "cuy," a traditional dish featuring roasted guinea pig. Considered a delicacy, cuy is crispy on the outside and tender on the inside, with a flavor likened to rabbit or dark meat chicken.

☐ **15.** Did you know that in some parts of the world, like Madagascar, people eat "honey ants"? These ants are filled with a sweet, honey-like substance and are considered a rare and delicious treat.

☐ **16.** "Stargazy pie" is a traditional Cornish dish featuring fish heads poking out from a pastry crust, appearing to gaze at the stars. It's said to have originated from a legend about a heroic fisherman and his catch during a famine.

☐ **17.** "Snake wine" is a beverage from Vietnam made by steeping whole venomous snakes in rice wine or grain alcohol. Believed to have medicinal properties, it's a potent and unusual drink.

☐ **18.** "Burong Isda" is a Filipino dish made from fermented rice and fish left to ferment for days until it develops a pungent aroma. Despite its strong smell, it's a beloved comfort food in some regions of the Philippines.

☐ **19.** In Scotland, you can find "haggis," a savory pudding made from sheep's heart, liver, and lungs, mixed with onions, oatmeal, and spices, all encased in a sheep's stomach.

☐ **20.** "Surströmming" is a Swedish delicacy of fermented Baltic sea herring. Its strong odor has led to it being banned on airlines and public transportation. Still, for some, the pungent flavor is a cherished part of Swedish cuisine.

☐ **21.** In certain regions of China, "chou doufu" or "stinky tofu" is a beloved street food made from fermented tofu. Its strong odor may be off-putting to some, but its crispy exterior and creamy interior have earned it a loyal following.

☐ **22.** "Laverbread" is a traditional Welsh dish made from edible seaweed, usually harvested from the coast. It's boiled for several hours, then minced or pureed, and often served with breakfast dishes like bacon and eggs.

☐ **23.** "Black pudding" is a type of blood sausage popular in the UK and Ireland, made from pork blood, fat, and oatmeal or barley. It's sliced and fried until crispy, often served as part of a complete breakfast.

☐ **24.** "Natto" is a traditional Japanese dish made from fermented soybeans. It has a strong, pungent smell and slimy texture, but its unique flavor and health benefits have made it a dietary staple for many.

☐ **25.** "Fried tarantulas" are a popular street food in Cambodia. These crunchy arachnids are seasoned with garlic and salt before being deep-fried to perfection, creating a crispy snack that's surprisingly tasty.

# **Vocabulary**Builder

Silkworm pupae (*See No. 5*) are the transitional stage between silkworm larvae and adult moths. During this phase, the silkworm spins a cocoon around itself using silk threads produced by special glands. Inside the cocoon, the pupa undergoes metamorphosis, transforming into a moth. In some cultures, silkworm pupae are consumed as a food delicacy.

# Chapter 30
# Curious Cultures

☐ **1.** In Iceland, books are exchanged as Christmas Eve presents, a cherished tradition called "Jólabókaflóð," which means "Christmas Book Flood."

☐ **2.** The Padaung women of Myanmar, also known as the "long-necked" tribe, wear brass coils around their necks from a young age, gradually lengthening them over time as a symbol of beauty and cultural identity.

☐ **3.** The Holi festival in India is a colorful celebration where people throw vibrant powders at each other to welcome the arrival of spring and to celebrate the triumph of good over evil.

☐ **4.** The San people of southern Africa communicate through a series of clicking sounds in their language, an integral part of their unique and ancient culture.

☐ 5. The Apatani women of India traditionally wear large nose plugs to deter raiding tribes from kidnapping them.

☐ **6.** In Ethiopia, the Surma tribe practices lip stretching, where women wear large lip plates as a symbol of beauty and identity.

☐ **7.** The Day of the Dead, or Día de los Muertos, is a vibrant Mexican holiday where families gather to honor and celebrate loved ones who have passed using colorful altars, marigold flowers, and sugar skulls.

☐ **8.** The Maasai of Kenya and Tanzania traditionally greet each other by spitting on their hands and shaking them.

☐ **9.** In Mongolia, it's customary to present guests with a bowl of airag, fermented mare's milk, as a gesture of hospitality.

☐ **10.** The Himba people of Namibia coat their skin and hair with a mixture of butterfat and ochre pigment, giving them a distinctive reddish appearance.

☐ **11.** On the Faroe Islands, an archipelago between Norway and Iceland, locals enjoy a traditional delicacy called "kiviak," which is made by fermenting whole seabirds inside a seal skin for several months.

☐ **12.** The Fulani people of West Africa are known for their elaborate hairstyles, which can signify wealth, status, age, and marital status.

☐ **13.** In Papua New Guinea, certain tribes engage in the practice of "sing-sing," where they showcase traditional music, dance, and elaborate body decorations during festivals.

☐ **14.** The Baining people of Papua New Guinea have a tradition of fire dancing, where men wear elaborate masks and dance barefoot over hot coals to welcome the new year.

☐ **15.** In South Korea, it's customary to celebrate a baby's first birthday with a ceremony called "Doljanchi." In this ceremony, the child is placed in front of various objects symbolizing different professions, and the one they grab predicts their future.

☐ **16.** The Nenets reindeer herders of Siberia migrate thousands of miles each year with their reindeer, braving extreme cold and harsh conditions.

☐ **17.** A "Despacho" is a ceremonial practice originating from the Andean regions of South America. It involves creating an offering bundle containing symbolic items such as food, flowers, and personal objects. The bundle is ritually blessed and often burned as an offering to spirits or the earth, expressing gratitude, seeking blessings, or marking significant life events.

☐ **18.** The Dogon people of Mali have a rich oral tradition and are known for their intricate knowledge of the stars and the cosmos, passed down through generations.

☐ **19.** In the Philippines, there's a unique festival called "Pahiyas," where houses are adorned with colorful decorations made from rice, fruits, and vegetables to honor the patron saint of farmers.

☐ **20.** In Bhutan, archery is not just a sport but a deeply ingrained cultural tradition, with competitions often accompanied by singing, dancing, and rituals.

☐ **21.** The Wodaabe tribe of Niger holds a unique beauty pageant for men called the "Gerewol," where participants dress elaborately, dance, and sing to attract potential partners.

☐ **22.** In Bolivia, there's a festival called "Alasitas," during which miniature items representing wealth and prosperity are bought and blessed in the hopes that they will come true in the coming year.

☐ **23.** The Bunun people of Taiwan have a tradition of polyphonic singing, where multiple singers produce harmonies and melodies simultaneously, creating a mesmerizing sound.

☐ **24.** In Nepal, there's a festival called "Gai Jatra," where people dress up in colorful costumes and parade the streets with cows to commemorate deceased loved ones.

☐ **25.** The Tsaatan reindeer herders of Mongolia live in teepee-like structures called "ortz," which they can quickly dismantle and relocate as they follow their reindeer herds.

# **Bonus**Facts

The Kalbelia tribe of India is skilled at snake charming and dancing. They perform intricate movements to the rhythm of traditional music while handling venomous snakes.

In Norway, there's a tradition called "Russefeiring," where high school graduates celebrate their final exams by dressing in elaborate costumes. The celebrations last for weeks and culminate on May 16.

The Inuit people of the Arctic have a tradition where they skillfully toss and manipulate a ball attached to a long string, showcasing their agility and dexterity.

# **Vocabulary**Builder

Polyphonic singing (*See No. 23*) is a musical style in which multiple independent vocal melodies harmonize simultaneously. Each voice maintains its unique rhythm and pitch, creating rich layers of sound. Common in various cultures worldwide, polyphonic singing showcases intricate interplay among singers, resulting in complex and harmonious compositions.

# NOTES

# NOTES

# Check out these other books by S.T. Frank

## STEM TRIVIA

### For Kids 10 & Up Who Love To Learn

**STEM Trivia For Kids 10 & Up Who Love To Learn** features 200 STEM Questions ranging from easy to challenging, STEM Word Search Puzzles, STEM Fast Facts, STEM Crossword Puzzles, and Much More!

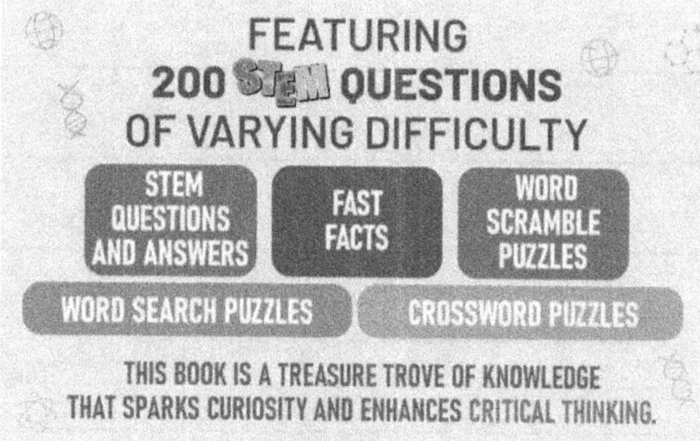


Available Only At Amazon.com

bit.ly/3UajpkJ

## Coloring Books

Available Only At Amazon.com

**Page 98**

# Check out these other books by S.T. Frank

## The All American Puzzle Book

Welcome to "The All American Puzzle Book" - a patriotic journey through the world of puzzles and trivia! This engaging collection offers a blend of classic and innovative challenges designed to entertain and inspire puzzle enthusiasts of all ages. Within these pages, you'll discover an array of brain-teasing delights, including patriotic Word Search, Crossword, Word Scramble, and Crypto-Quote puzzles, alongside the beloved Mazes and Sudoku.

Available Only At Amazon.com
https://amzn.to/4aMo9Sl

---

## Coloring Books

Available Only At Amazon.com

# Check out these other books by S.T. Frank

## Earth & Beyond
### For Kids 10 & Up Who Love To Learn

Welcome to the Amazing Earth & Beyond Activity Book For Kids 10 & Up Who Love To Learn! Embark on an engaging and educational journey through the wonders of our planet and beyond. This engaging activity book is designed to captivate young minds and inspire a passion for exploration and discovery. Divided into four fascinating sections, we delve into the mysteries of The Continents, The Oceans, Weather & Climate, and Beyond Earth.

Available Only At Amazon.com
https://amzn.to/3TmzFOM

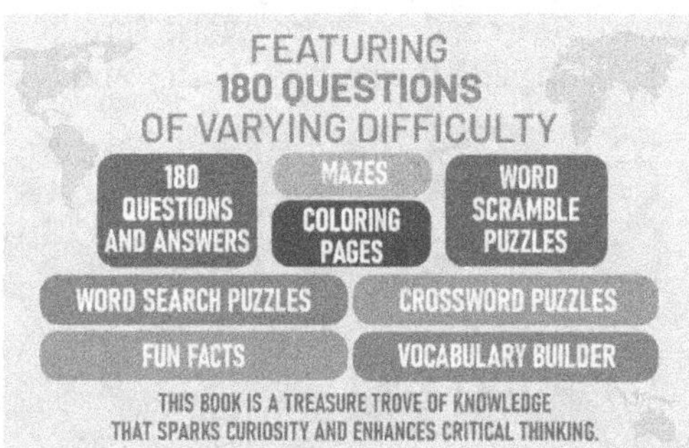


---

## Word Search Puzzles
### For Adults & Seniors

Welcome to the ultimate Word Search Puzzle Book, where words come alive in a labyrinth of letters waiting to be discovered! With 3,000 carefully selected words spanning across 125 captivating themed puzzles, this book promises an endless adventure for word enthusiasts of all ages and skill levels. Whether you're a beginner looking for a relaxing brain exercise or a seasoned puzzler seeking a challenge, there's something here for everyone.

Available Only At Amazon.com
https://amzn.to/49wkc46

# Check out these other books by S.T. Frank

## Amazing Animals

### For Kids 8 & Up Who Love To Learn

Welcome to the captivating world of the **"Amazing Animals Activity Book For Kids 8 & Up Who Love To Learn."** Embark on an exciting journey through the animal kingdom with a book designed to engage young minds and foster a love for learning. This immersive activity book is divided into four enriching chapters.

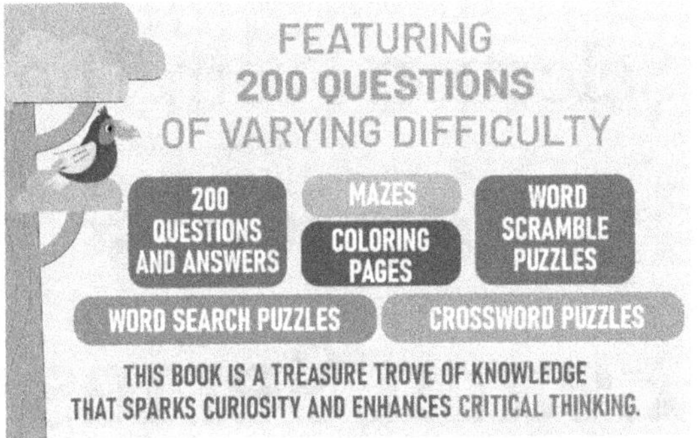

Available Only At Amazon.com
https://amzn.to/3HJv8ix

# S.T. Frank Books

To See The Complete Selection From The

## Activity Books For Kids
## Who Love To Learn Series

And The

## Brain Games For Adults
## And Seniors Series

Go To:

# www.stfrankbooks.com